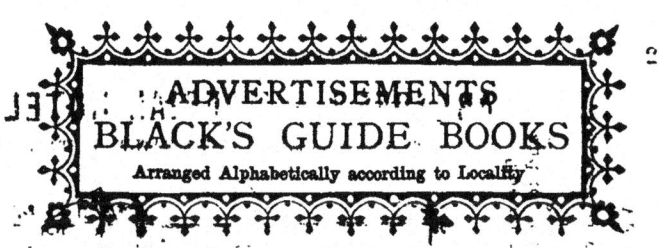

ADVERTISEMENTS
BLACK'S GUIDE BOOKS
Arranged Alphabetically according to Locality

SUMMER TOURS IN SCOTLAND.
GLASGOW AND THE HIGHLANDS.
(Royal Route via Crinan and Caledonian Canals.)

Special Tourist Cabin Tickets issued during the Season,
For One Week, £3 ; or Two Weeks, £5.
Giving the *privilege* of the run of *all the undernamed Steamers to any part
of the Highlands* where they may call at during the time specified.
Breakfast, Dinner, and Tea for One Week, £2 additional.

THE				MAIL
ROYAL				STEAMERS

CLAYMORE (New Screw Steamship)

COLUMBA	ISLAY	GLENCOE	INVERARAY	CASTLE
IONA	CHEVALIER	GONDOLIER	STAFFA	FINGAL
MOUNTAINEER	PIONEER	GLENGARRY	LINNET	LOCHIEL
CLANSMAN	CLYDESDALE	CYGNET	PLOVER	LOCHAWE

AND QUEEN OF THE LAKE.

Sail during the season for Port Ellen, Port Askaig, Islay, Oban, Fort-
William, Inverness, Staffa, Iona, Glencoe, Loch Awe, Tobermory, Portree,
Strome Ferry, Gairloch, Ullapool, Lochinver, Lochmaddy, Tarbert, Harris,
and Stornoway ; affording Tourists an opportunity of visiting the Magni-
ficent Scenery of Loch Awe, Glencoe, the Coolin Hills, Loch Coruisk,
Loch Maree, and the famed Islands of Staffa and Iona.

. These vessels afford in their passage a view of the beautiful scenery of the Clyde,
with all its Watering-Places—the Island and Kyles of Bute—Island of Arran—Mountains of Cowal, Knapdale, and Kintyre—Lochfyne—Crinan—with the Islands of Jura,
Scarba, Mull, and many others of the Western Sea—The Whirlpool of Corryvreckan—
the Mountains of Lorn, of Morven, of Appin, of Kingairloch, and Ben Nevis—Inver-
lochy—The Lands of Lochiel, the scene of the wanderings of Prince Charles, and near
to where the clans raised his Standard in the '45—Lochaber—the Caledonian Canal—
Loch Lochy—Loch Oich—Loch Ness, with the Glens and Mountains on either side, and
the celebrated FALLS OF FOYERS. From Ardrishaig to Ford, the route passes
through the picturesque valley of Kilmartin and by Kilmartin Castle, Carnassarie
Castle, Bull's Pass, Dog's Head Loch, and Ederline Loch. The attractions on Loch
Awe are numerous. There are twenty-four Islands, many of them richly wooded, and
crowned by the ruins of four Castles and two Monasteries. At the foot of the Lake is
the romantic Pass of Brander, where MacDougall of Lorne encountered the Bruce, and
where Ben Cruachan rises 3800 feet from the Awe. Books descriptive of the route may
be had on board the Steamers. Official Guide Book, 2d. ; Illustrated, 3d. ; Cloth, 1s.
Time-Bill, with Map and Tourist Fares, sent post free on application to the
Proprietor, DAVID MACBRAYNE, 119 Hope Street, Glasgow

GLASGOW, 1881.

A

ABERDEEN.

MANN'S PALACE HOTEL,
UNION STREET AND BRIDGE STREET.

The Hotel Bus awaits the arrival of all through Trains.

THE PALACE is the most recently erected and only First-class Hotel in the City. The Management being under the direct and constant supervision of the proprietor, who has had a long practical experience, and as *Chef de Cuisine* has had the honour of serving personally many of the Royal and Imperial Families of Europe, he trusts to merit the patronage of visitors.

LETTERS AND TELEGRAMS PROMPTLY ATTENDED TO.

Position, the most central and select, though only One Hundred Yards from the Railway Station. CHARLES MANN, *Proprietor.*

GRAND
PUMP ROOM HOTEL

Is situated in the centre of the City, and connected with the finest suite of Mineral Water Baths in Europe,

IMMEDIATELY OPPOSITE THE GRAND PUMP ROOM AND ABBEY.

This Handsome Hotel is replete with every accommodation, and is especially adapted for those requiring the use of the Bath Waters.

The Wines are carefully selected, and the Cuisine is under an experienced Chef.

FOR PARTICULARS APPLY TO

C. W. RADWAY, *Lessee.*

BELFAST.

ROBINSON'S COMMERCIAL TEMPERANCE HOTEL

82 DONEGALL STREET

ESTABLISHED 1851.

A FIRST-CLASS Family and Commercial Hotel. Conducted on strictly Abstinence Principles. Comfort, Quiet, and moderate Charges.

Private Sitting Rooms and Show Rooms.

BETTWS-Y-COED.

ROYAL OAK HOTEL

THIS Hotel has an unrivalled situation, and is very suitable as a centre from which the most beautiful scenery in North Wales may be visited. It is near the Station, to which it has a private road. The coaches for Llanberis, Beddgelert, and Bangor start daily from the Hotel.

AN OMNIBUS MEETS EVERY TRAIN.

FISHING TICKETS FOR ALL THE NEIGHBOURING RIVERS.

Billiards.   Lawn Tennis.   Archery.

POSTING IN ALL ITS BRANCHES.

David Cox's celebrated Signboard Picture.

E. PULLAN, *Proprietor* (Ten Years Proprietor of the Crown Hotel, Harrogate).

BLAIR-ATHOLE.

ATHOLE ARMS HOTEL.

Adjoining the Railway Station. No Omnibus necessary.

THE recently completed additions render this Hotel one of the largest and best appointed in the Highlands, while this year, by further refurnishing in the first style, no expense has been spared to enhance its reputation.

TABLE D'HÔTE daily during the season in the well-known magnificent Dining Hall, with which is connected *en suite* a spacious and elegantly furnished Drawing-Room.

Special terms for Board by the week, except during August.

Blair-Athole is much the nearest and most central point from which to visit Killiecrankie, the Queen's View, Loch Tummel, Rannoch, Glen Tilt, Braemar; the Falls of Bruar, Garry, Tummel, and Fender; the grounds of Blair Castle, &c.; and it is the most convenient resting-place for breaking the long railway journey to and from the North of Scotland.

THE POSTING DEPARTMENT is thoroughly well equipped.

Experienced Guides and Ponies for Glen Tilt, Braemar, and Mountain Excursions.

D. & R. T. MACDONALD, *Proprietors.*

THE FIFE ARMS HOTEL

BRAEMAR, BY BALMORAL.

Patronised by Royal Family and Court.

MR. M'NAB begs respectfully to inform the Nobility, Gentry, and Tourists, that the extensive additions to the Hotel are now completed. The Hotel, as now constructed, comprises over 100 Bedrooms, a Dining Saloon (one of the largest and most elegant in Scotland), elegant Private Sitting-Rooms, Ladies' Drawing-Room, Billiard-Room, and Bath-Rooms.

Charges strictly moderate. Letters or Telegrams will receive the most careful attention. Posting in all its varied departments. Coaches during the Season daily from the hotel to Blairgowrie and Dunkeld, and twice daily between Ballater and Braemar.

Parties Boarded by the Week or Month.

NOTE.—*Gentlemen staying at the Hotel can have excellent Salmon or Trout Fishing.*

BRAEMAR.

THE INVERCAULD ARMS,

The finest Hotel situation in Scotland.

Recently re-erected after Plans by J. T. WIMPERIS, Esq., Sackville St., London.

MAGNIFICENT DINING HALL, ELEGANT LADIES' DRAWING ROOM, AND NUMEROUS SUITES OF APARTMENTS.

POSTING IN ALL ITS BRANCHES.

Coaches during the Season to Blairgowrie, Dunkeld, and Ballater.

Excellent Salmon Fishing in connection with the Hotel.

Letters and Telegrams Punctually attended to.

A. M'GREGOR.

(IRELAND) INTERNATIONAL HOTEL, BRAY,

County Wicklow.

THIS FIRST-CLASS HOTEL is situated near the Railway Station, Sea-beach, and Esplanade, central to all the far-famed Scenery of the County of Wicklow.

Visitors to this fashionable place will find THE INTERNATIONAL HOTEL replete with every comfort, and the *Cuisine* and Wines of the best quality.

All Charges are fixed and moderate.

Boarding Terms per week may be had on application to the MANAGER.

C. DUFRESNE, *Proprietor.*

BRIDGE OF ALLAN.

QUEEN'S HOTEL.

This Hotel affords excellent accommodation for Tourists and Visitors.

The Hotel 'bus meets all Trains.

A. ANDERSON, *Proprietor.*

HYDROPATHIC ESTABLISHMENT.

BRIDGE OF ALLAN, NEAR STIRLING.

THE situation is high and dry, cool in summer and mild in winter. The House is well appointed, and the Baths are elegant and complete.

Terms, including all charges, £2 : 12 : 6 per week.

Applications to be addressed to Mr. M'KAY, House Superintendent.

BUXTON, DERBYSHIRE.

CRESCENT HOTEL.

THIS FIRST-CLASS HOTEL for FAMILIES and GENTLEMEN forms the South Wing of the Crescent. It is only ONE MINUTE from RAILWAY STATIONS, and is connected by Covered Colonnade with the Hot and Natural Baths, Drinking Wells, and the New Pavilion and Gardens, where a splendid BAND performs Four Hours daily.

THE ASSEMBLY ROOM

in this Hotel, which has long been celebrated for its elegant proportions, has recently been redecorated in the first style, and is now converted into the

DINING-ROOM OF THE HOTEL.

Public, Dining, Drawing, Smoking, and Billiard Rooms.

SUITES OF APARTMENTS FOR PRIVATE FAMILIES.

TABLE D'HOTE AT 6 P.M.

FIRST-CLASS STABLING AND LOCK-UP COACH-HOUSES.

JOHN SMILTER, *Proprietor.*

CALLANDER.

THE M'GREGOR HOTEL.

ALEXANDER M'NAUGHTON, PROPRIETOR

(For Ten Years Waiter at the Alexandra Hotel, Oban).

TOURISTS and Families visiting the above long-established and First-Class Hotel will have every comfort and attention, and the Charges will be found strictly moderate.

Salmon and Trout Fishing on several Lochs, also on three miles of the River Teith.

Letters and Telegrams for Rooms promptly attended to.

CARLISLE.

THE COUNTY AND STATION HOTEL,

FOR Families and Gentlemen, is connected with the Platform of the Central Railway Station by a covered way. Porters from this Hotel are in attendance on arrival of all Trains.

A Ladies' Coffee-Room.

CARNARVON, NORTH WALES.

THE ROYAL HOTEL

(LATE UXBRIDGE ARMS),

FIRST-CLASS FAMILY & COMMERCIAL ESTABLISHMENT

Beautifully situated on the Banks of the Menai Straits, and in close proximity to the Railway Station.

EDWARD HUMPHREYS.

An Omnibus will regularly attend the arrival of each Train at the Railway Station. Billiards in detached premises.

On and after June 19th, a Coach round Snowdon, after the arrival of the 9.25 a.m. train, *via* Beddgelert, Vale of Gwynant, and the Pass of Llanberis, arriving at the hotel for dinner, and in time for the train for Llandudno, Rhyl, &c.

B

CHATSWORTH HOTEL, EDENSOR,
DERBYSHIRE.

This Hotel is beautifully situated in Chatsworth Park, and within ten minutes' walk of the princely residence of the Duke of Devonshire.

The hotel is the largest in the neighbourhood, and its proximity to the Bowsley Station, on the Midland Railway, affords every facility to Tourists desirous of visiting the beauties of Haddon Hall, Matlock, the Mines at Castleton, Dove Dale, etc.

Omnibuses from the hotel meet all the principal trains at Rowsley Station.

A spacious Coffee-Room for Ladies.   Private Sitting and well-appointed Bed-Rooms. Post-horses, etc.

HENRY HARRISON, Proprietor;
IN CONNECTION WITH ST. ANN'S HOTEL, BUXTON.
Railway Station, Rowsley.   *Postal address,* Bakewell.
— Day Tickets for the Chatsworth Fishery. —

CHESTER.

THE GROSVENOR HOTEL,

FIRST-CLASS.   Situated in the centre of the City, close to the Cathedral and other objects of interest.

A Large Coffee-Room and Ladies' Drawing Room for the convenience of Ladies and Families. The Bedrooms are large and handsomely furnished.

Open and close Carriages, and Posting in all its Branches.

Omnibuses attend the Trains for the use of Visitors to the Hotel.   Tariff to be had on application.   A Night Porter in attendance.

DAVID FOSTER, *Manager.*

CLIFTON DOWN HOTEL.
CLIFTON, NEAR BRISTOL.

THIS Hotel is within two hours and a half from London, by the Great Western Rail, per Flying Dutchman (the fastest train in the world). The situation of the hotel is unrivalled, being on the Downs, and facing the Suspension Bridge, St. Vincent's Rocks, and Nightingale Valley. Tourists should not miss seeing this truly grand and bold scenery. Visitors will find every comfort and Quietude ; and those proceeding to Ilfracombe should take Clifton on their route, and save the long and tedious journey by South Western. The hotel is noted for its extensive Wine List, and its Moderate charges. A private Omnibus meets all the express and principal trains.

N.B.—From this hotel the following TRIPS are easy, returning to the hotel the same day :—Chepstow Castle, the Wynd Cliff, Tintern Abbey, Wells Cathedral, Glastonbury, Tor, Bath, Weston-super-Mare, Clevedon, Portishead, Cardiff, Newport, and Channel Docks.

All communications address,
Clifton Hotel Company (Limited).   D. GITTINS, *Manager.*

CONWAY.

THE CASTLE HOTEL.

FIRST-CLASS.   Beautifully situated in the Vale of Conway, and very central for Tourists in North Wales.

COLWYN BAY, NORTH WALES.

PWLLYCROCHON HOTEL,

(Late the Residence of Lady Erskine).

THIS First-class Family Hotel is most beautifully situated in its own finely-wooded park in Colwyn Bay, commanding splendid land and sea views; there are miles of delightful walks in the adjacent woods. It is within a few minutes' walk of the Beach and ten minutes' of Colwyn Bay Station, and a short drive of Conway and Llandudno.

Sea-Bathing, Billiards, Posting.

J. PORTER, Proprietor.

CORK.

STEPHENS' COMMERCIAL HOTEL

(Opposite the General Post Office, Cork).

POSSESSES first-class accommodation for Tourists, Commercial Gentlemen, and Families.

It is very centrally situated, being opposite the General Post Office—close to the Bank, Theatre, &c. &c.

Charges extremely Moderate.

WILLIAM D. STEPHENS, PROPRIETOR,
From the West of England.

EXTRACT from a " Tour through Ireland," published in the *North Briton*, 1864 :—

" When we arrived in Cork we took up our quarters at Stephens' Commercial Hotel, where we obtained excellent accommodation.

" What this Hotel lacks in external show is amply compensated by unremitting attention on the part of the Proprietors and their attendants to the comfort of their Guests."

IMPERIAL  HOTEL.

CORK.

P. CURRY, Proprietor,

THIS long-established and well-known Hotel is conducted on the most approved and modern system. It possesses every requisite to promote the Comfort and Convenience of Tourists. The Hotel contains

OVER ONE HUNDRED BEDROOMS,

Three Coffee Rooms, Commercial Room, a Drawing Room for Ladies and Families, Suites of Private Apartments, Smoking and Billiard Rooms, Bath Rooms, &c.

TABLE D'HOTE DAILY AT HALF-PAST SIX O'CLOCK.

The Hotel adjoins the General Post Office; as also the Commercial Building, where Merchants meet on "'Change," and the earliest Telegraphic News is received, to the Reading Room, of which Visitors to the Hotel have free access. It has been patronised within the last few years by their Royal Highnesses the Prince of Wales, Duke of Connaught, Prince Alfred, Prince Napoleon, the Duc D'Orleans, the Comte de Paris, and the Count de Flandres, the successive Lords-Lieutenant of Ireland—Clarendon, Eglinton, Carlisle, Abercorn, and Marlborough—as well as by the Nobility, and most of the leading Gentry visiting Cork.

The Charges will be found most Moderate.

The Imperial Omnibuses attend the arrival and departure of each Train.

Extract from Sir CUSACK RONEY'S "Month in Ireland:"

"Judge Haliburton (Sam Slick) says, 'There are two things to be recommended to the notice of visitors to Ireland:—If you are an admirer of beautiful scenery, go to the Cove of Cork; if you want a good hotel, go to the Imperial.' The Hotel in question is situated in Pembroke Street, having an entrance also in the South Mall, through the Commercial Buildings," the splendid News Room of which is open to visitors to the Hotel. For convenience and comfort there is not a hotel superior to it in the Empire."

DUBLIN.

SHELBOURNE HOTEL

SITUATED in most central and fashionable part of Dublin, and is the great Tourist Hotel of Ireland. Contains magnificent Public Rooms, Elevator, Telegraph Office, &c. &c. First-Class. Charges Moderate.

JURY & COTTON, Proprietors.

DUBLIN.

SALT HILL HOTEL
MONKSTOWN, CO. DUBLIN.

FIRST-Class Hotel for Families and Gentlemen. Pleasantly situated in its own grounds (twenty minutes by rail from Dublin). Elegantly furnished suites of apartments, spacious Coffee, Reception, and Drawing Rooms, facing the sea. An excellent Billiard Room, provided with a champion Billiard Table; Lawn Tennis and Croquet Grounds. Table d'Hote. Carriages in every variety. The whole under the personal superintendence of the Proprietor, WILLIAM PARRY.

N.B.—Special arrangements for families sojourning.

DUNKELD.

THE DUKE OF ATHOLE'S ARMS HOTEL
ROBERTSON, <i>Proprietor (late GRANT).</i>

THIS Hotel, from its situation close to the beautiful Bridge of Dunkeld, commands an unrivalled view of the magnificent scenery on either side of the River Tay. The Apartments, both public and Private, are elegantly furnished and well aired.

Her Majesty the Queen, in her Journal of her Life in the Highlands, has been graciously pleased to take notice of this Hotel as being very clean, and having such a charming view from the windows. The Empress of the French, with her Son, the Prince Imperial, also visited this Hotel, and was pleased to express her entire approval of all the arrangements. EVERY ATTENTION IS PAID TO THE COMFORT OF VISITORS. Job and Post Horses, with Careful Drivers. An Omnibus awaits the arrival of all the Trains.

Seats can be secured at this Hotel for the Braemar Coach.

DUNOON.

THE CROWN HOTEL
(Situated close to the Pier.)

THIS first-class Hotel has been lately enlarged and refurnished, and Tourists and Travelling Public will find every comfort, combined with moderate charges. Dunoon, by its mild climate, is recommended for a Winter Residence, and the "Crown" offers every comfort. Full Board, 50s. per week.

Hot and Cold Sea Water Baths. Table d'Hote Daily,

OSCAR TROEGER, Proprietor.

DUNBLANE HYDROPATHIC ESTABLISHMENT.

THIS MAGNIFICENT ESTABLISHMENT, built on a commanding eminence facing the Grampian Hills, and in close proximity to Dunblane Railway Station, offers to Tourists and Travellers all the Luxuries and Conveniences of a First-Class Metropolitan Hotel, and to parties requiring rest and change all the comforts and appliances (including the most skilled Medical Treatment) of the best English Hydropathic Institutions,—all combined with the most Moderate Charges.

Situated in the very centre of Scotland, at the entrance to the Highlands of Perthshire, Dunblane is an Important Railway Junction on the Main Line between England and the North of Scotland, about one hour from Edinburgh, Glasgow, Perth, or Dundee, and forms a most convenient stopping place for parties travelling to or from Perthshire, Argyllshire, Inverness-shire, and Aberdeenshire.

The Branch-line to the Trossachs, Killin, Oban, Inveraray, and the West Highlands, leaves the main line at Dunblane: and Travellers stopping at Dunblane can break the journey there without extra charge.

The Coupons issued by the Railway Company are accepted in the Establishment. Private Sitting-rooms, Superb Public Drawing-room, Ladies' Room, Dining-room, Billiard-room, and large Recreation-room 120 feet long, where Visitors may find amusement in wet weather.

A complete system of Baths free to Visitors.

An Omnibus meets the arrival and departure of all trains between 8 A.M. and 8.37 P.M.

The scenery around Dunblane is unsurpassed in Scotland, and the neighbourhood abounds in magnificent Walks and Drives. The following trips can be easily made, returning to the Establishment the same day :—The Trossachs, Loch Lomond, Edinburgh, Glasgow, Perth, Stirling Castle, Doune Castle, Field of Bannockburn, Castle Campbell, Rumbling Bridge, Roman Camp at Ardoch, the most perfect Roman Camp in Britain, &c. &c.

The charges for driving are very moderate, and the roads are free of Tolls.

EDINBURGH.
PHILP'S COCKBURN HOTEL,

Immediately adjoining the terminus of the Midland and Great Northern Trains, Waverley Bridge Station.

THIS commodious and well-known Hotel is beautifully situated, overlooking PRINCES STREET GARDENS, and commanding some of the finest views of the City.

(*In connection with Philp's Cockburn Hotel, Glasgow.*)

Excellent Turkish and other Baths in both Hotels.

Charges, including Attendance, strictly Moderate.

N.B.—Mr. Cook (of London) makes this Hotel his headquarters when in Scotland, where every information may be obtained of his Tourist arrangements, and Tickets for Highland and other Tours supplied.

GLASGOW.
PHILP'S COCKBURN HOTEL,
141 BATH STREET.

THE COCKBURN HOTEL, containing upwards of 100 Rooms, is specially planned and constructed with every Modern Improvement to meet the requirements of a First-Class Hotel. Situated in an elevated and quiet, but central and convenient part of the City; within easy access of the different Railway Stations and Steam-Ship Landings. Street Cars pass within a few yards to all parts of the City.

A Passenger Elevator to every landing.

Agent for Cook's System of Tours to the Highlands and Islands of Scotland, and Tickets supplied same as at the Edinburgh House.

Both Hotels conducted on the *same principles.*

(One of the finest Hotels in Europe.)

THE

ROYAL HOTEL

DONALD MACGREGOR, Proprietor,

53 PRINCES STREET, EDINBURGH.

The Royal Hotel is within a hundred yards of Railway Terminus, and occupies the finest position in the City.

PLACES OF INTEREST SEEN FROM HOTEL:— Arthur's Seat, over 800 feet high. Assembly Hall Calton Hill. Edinburgh Castle. East and West Princes Street Gardens. Free Church College and Assembly Hall. Royal Observatory. Sir Walter Scott's Monument. Salisbury Crags. St. Giles's Cathedral. Parliament House. The Royal Institution. The Royal Scottish Academy and National Gallery. The Antiquarian Museum. From tower of Hotel are seen the Firth of Forth, Bass Rock, the Lomond, Corstorphine, and Pentland Hills, and a part of four or five of the neighbouring counties.

Charges Moderate. Rooms from 2s. 6d. Passenger Elevator. Night Porters.

CAUTION.—Visitors intending to put up at the Royal must be careful to see that they are taken there, as mistakes have occurred causing great disappointment.

CRANSTON'S OLD

WAVERLEY

TEMPERANCE HOTEL,

43 PRINCES STREET, EDINBURGH.

ROBERT CRANSTON, in returning thanks to his numerous Friends and the Public, begs to inform them that the above Hotel has been reconstructed, fitted, and furnished with all the most modern improvements which the present times can supply, and that, notwithstanding the great rise in the value of property in Princes Street, and the high prices of labour and material in the erection of his New Hotel, the charges for Bed-Rooms remain the same as they were 33 years ago. Hoping for a continuance of their kind patronage, R. C. will make it his constant endeavour to attend to the comfort, convenience, and interest of his Friends.

TO STRANGERS unacquainted with Edinburgh, R. C. begs to intimate that the situation of the OLD WAVERLEY is within one minute from the Great Central Railway Station, and commands the Grandest Views in the City; while the street itself is said to be the finest in the world. Immediately opposite the Hotel, and forming the south side of Princes Street, is the Garden Terrace, a public promenade, upon which stand the unequalled "Scott" and other noble monuments, while the gardens below form the valley betwixt the Old and New Towns. To the west, the grand old Castle, towering over the city; to the south, the romantic Old Town, with St. Giles's Cathedral and other prominent structures; and to the east, Arthur's Seat, Holyrood Palace, and Calton Hill, the view from the latter of which is said to surpass even that of the Bay of Naples.

Uniform Charges are made at the following Hotels, belonging to the same Proprietor:—

EDINBURGH	OLD WAVERLEY, 43 PRINCES STREET.
EDINBURGH	NEW WAVERLEY, 18 WATERLOO PLACE.
GLASGOW	185 BUCHANAN STREET.
LONDON	4 LAWRENCE LANE, CHEAPSIDE.

Breakfast or Tea	1s. 3d., 1s. 6d., 1s. 9d.
Public Dinner	2s.
Bed-Room	1s. 6d.
Private Parlours	2s.
Service	1s.

THE NEW WAVERLEY, Waterloo Place, contains numerous and commodious Stock-Rooms on the ground-floor, well suited for all kinds of Commercial Merchandise. Also a large Hall on the ground-floor, seated for about 700 people, for Public Meetings, Concerts, &c.

Recommended by Bradshaw's Tourists' Guide as "the cheapest and best Temperance Hotel they had ever seen," and by J. B. Gough as "the only Home he had found saving his own in America."

DARLING'S REGENT HOTEL,
20 WATERLOO PLACE, EDINBURGH.

Nearly opposite the General Post-Office, and only a few minutes' walk from General Railway Terminus.

This is admitted to be one of the best Temperance Hotels in Scotland.

EDINBURGH.

THE LONDON HOTEL
ST. ANDREW SQUARE, EDINBURGH.

Established upwards of Fifty Years.   *Patronised by Royalty.*

A Commodious and Comfortable Hotel, most conveniently situated.

Proprietor, **HENRY WHITE**, late Clubmaster to the University Club.

VEITCH'S
PRIVATE HOTEL,
127-133 GEORGE STREET, EDINBURGH.

Charges strictly Moderate.   Coffee-Room.

CATHERINE VEITCH & SON, Proprietors.

THE ROYAL ALEXANDRA HOTEL
11, 12, & 13 SHANDWICK PLACE, EDINBURGH.

West End of Princes Street, and in the immediate neighbourhood of the Caledonian and Haymarket Stations.

THIS First-class Family Hotel was opened on the 1st of June 1874 by MISS BROWN, formerly of the Windsor Hotel, Moray Place, and the Clarendon Hotel, Princes Street. The ROYAL ALEXANDRA HOTEL has been entirely rebuilt, and fitted up with every modern improvement required for the convenience and comfort of visitors, and MISS BROWN hopes to merit a continuance of the favours she has already received. Coffee-room and public Drawing-room.

ELGIN.

ELGIN STATION HOTEL.

THIS comfortable and commodious House occupies one of the best sites in the town, is close to both the railway stations, within five minutes' walk of the fine ruins of the cathedral, and within an easy drive of the beautiful and romantic Pluscarden Abbey and other places of interest in the neighbourhood. It is newly furnished in the best style, and contains suites of private rooms, Commercial, Coffee, and Drawing Rooms, large Dining Hall and Stock Rooms, Smoking Room, Billiard Room, and Bath Room; numerous Bedrooms.

Letters and Telegrams promptly attended to.

Table d'Hôte daily during the season.

WILLIAM CHRISTIE, *Lessee.*

EXETER.

ROYAL CLARENCE HOTEL,

CATHEDRAL YARD.

WITH FULL VIEW OF THE GRAND OLD CATHEDRAL.

FIRST CLASS HOTEL. REDUCED CHARGES.

Every effort is made to ensure the unqualified satisfaction of Ladies and Gentlemen.

Handsomely Furnished Suites of Apartments.

LADIES' COFFEE ROOM.   HOT AND COLD BATHS.

Omnibuses and Cabs meet every Train.

J. HEADON STANBURY, *Proprietor.*

FALMOUTH.

GREEN BANK HOTEL.

THIS HOTEL is beautifully situated, facing the Harbour, Pendennis, and St. Mawes Castle, and is replete with every comfort for Families and Gentlemen. Very convenient for Boating and Fishing, there being a landing pier adjoining the House.   LADIES' COFFEE ROOM.

Billiard Room. Posting in all its Branches. Charges Moderate.

The Hotel Omnibus meets all Trains.

Suites of Rooms reserved on application to the Proprietor, J. H. MITCHELL.

Omnibus to and from the Lizard daily.

FALMOUTH.

CARTER'S ROYAL HOTEL

THIS FIRST-CLASS HOTEL is centrally situated for business or pleasure. The apartments are beautifully furnished.

HANDSOME COFFEE-ROOM AND LADIES' DRAWING-ROOM.

The scenery of this neighbourhood is unsurpassed. The Royal River Fal being unrivalled. Good bathing beaches. Omnibuses for the Lizard, &c., start from and arrive at this Hotel.

Moderate and fixed charges.   Tariffs forwarded.

RICHARD CARTER, *Proprietor.*

THE SHANDON HYDROPATHIC

BEAUTIFULLY SITUATED ON THE GARELOCH, near HELENSBURGH.

Terms, £3 : 3s. per week, or 10s. 6d. per day.

THE FINEST HYDROPATHIC RESIDENCE IN THE KINGDOM.

WELL sheltered, salubrious climate, Highland Scenery, within easy drives to Lochlong and Lochlomond. The Conservatory, Vineries, Gardens, and Policies, with five miles of Enclosed Gravel Walks, are unrivalled. Large Salt Water Swimming, Turkish and other Baths, with every Modern luxury. Pleasure Boats, &c. Post and Telegraph Offices at the Entrance Lodge. Resident Physician—Dr. F. F. JAY.

Omnibus awaits arrival of 10.40 and 4.5 Trains from Glasgow.

Apply to the Manager, West Shandon, by Helensburgh.

CAMPBELL'S ROYAL
STATION HOTEL
FORRES, Adjoining the Railway Platform.
(Patronised by the Royal Family and Leading Members of the Nobility and Aristocracy of Europe.)
APARTMENTS EN SUITE.   SPACIOUS BILLIARD & SMOKING ROOM.
Boots in attendance at all Trains.

JAMES CAMPBELL, *Proprietor and Lessee.*

THE BATH HOTEL,
152 BATH STREET.
The most comfortable First-class Hotel in Glasgow.   Very moderate charges.

P. ROBERTSON, PROPRIETOR.

GLASGOW.

ATHOLE ARMS HOTEL
(Opposite North British Railway),
21 DUNDAS STREET.

ALEXANDER GOW has the pleasure of announcing that he resumes the Occupancy and Management of this favourite Hotel, and trusts, by giving the same care and attention, to receive the liberal patronage he formerly enjoyed.

The ample accommodation and conveniences of the Hotel are well known, and under Mr. Gow's personal superintendence, will be used to the best advantage of his customers.

DINNER AND SUPPER PARTIES
(for which the Hotel is admirably adapted) will receive special attention.

ALEXANDER GOW, *Proprietor.*

THE GRAND HOTEL,

CHARING CROSS, GLASGOW.

THIS magnificent Hotel, the comfort of which has been greatly increased by the extensive and costly alterations just completed, is now open for the reception of families and gentlemen under new and efficient management. This establishment offers unrivalled accommodation to visitors during their stay in Glasgow, whether for one day, or for a lengthened period.

The charges are strictly moderate, and the attendance all that can be desired.

Letters and Telegrams to be addressed to

W. C. DAVIDSON, *Manager.*

BLAIR'S HOTEL,

80 BATH STREET, GLASGOW.

THIS New First-Class TEMPERANCE HOTEL, situated within four minutes' walk of the Principal Railway Stations, is unsurpassed for Cleanliness, Quiet, and Comfort.

Private Parlours and Stock Rooms.

BREAKFAST,	DINNER,	BED ROOM,	ATTENDANCE,
1s. 6d. 1s. 9d.	2s. From 1s. 6d.	1s. 6d.	1s.

THE ROYAL HOTEL,

GEORGE SQUARE, GLASGOW.

OPPOSITE THE GENERAL POST OFFICE.

All Communications to be addressed to the Manager.

Noted House for Scotch Goods.

NEILSON, SHAW, AND MACGREGOR,
44 BUCHANAN STREET, GLASGOW,
SILK MERCERS, LINEN AND WOOLLEN DRAPERS,
SHAWL IMPORTERS, AND GENERAL WAREHOUSEMEN.

DEPARTMENTS—

British and Foreign Silks.	Clan and Fancy Tartans.
French and Paisley Shawls.	Scotch and English Tweeds.
Real Shetland Shawls.	Real Aberdeen Winceys.

Hosiery.	Prints.	Grenadines.	Ribbons.	Linens.
Gloves.	Bareges.	Paramattas.	Flowers.	
Parasols.	Alpaccas.	Knitting Yarns.	Feathers.	
Merinoes.	Muslins.	Trimmings.	Laces.	
Coburgs.	Cambrics.	Small Wares.	Furs.	Blankets.

A LARGE SALOON FOR MANTLES, MILLINERY, LADIES' OUTFIT, ETC.
MARRIAGE TROUSSEAUX OF THE BEST MATERIALS AND WORKMANSHIP.

UPHOLSTERY DEPARTMENT.
CARPETS, OIL CLOTHS, WINDOW CORNICES, AND CURTAIN FABRICS,
SCOTCH SHEETINGS, TABLE LINEN, ETC.

A FULL STOCK OF SUMMER COSTUMES
READY MADE, OR MADE TO ORDER IN A FEW HOURS' NOTICE,
For Coast and Travelling Season.

FAMILY MOURNINGS.
The Best Materials supplied in all the Departments.
A Competent Person sent to Residences in Town or Country to take instructions when required.

TAILORING DEPARTMENT.
FOR GENTLEMEN'S and BOYS' SUITS.
A Large Variety of Scotch, English, and German Tweeds, Heather Mixtures, etc.,
always in Stock.
SHOOTING COATS, WATER COATS, HIGHLAND CAPES, ETC.,
Made to Order on the shortest notice.
A FIRST-CLASS CUTTER ON THE PREMISES.
This NEW DEPARTMENT applies also to LADIES' JACKETS, RIDING HABITS,
COSTUMES, BODICES, and to MINISTERS' GOWNS and CASSOCKS.

TO TOURISTS.

Tourists will find a large variety of

STEREOSCOPIC, SCRAP, AND

VIEWS OF SCOTTISH SCENERY,

GUIDE BOOKS, MAPS, &c., &c.,

AT

REID'S STATIONERY EMPORIUM,

144 ARGYLE STREET, GLASGOW, 144.

Fourth Shop West of Buchanan Street.

Visitors are invited to Inspect the Stock, though they may not wish to Purchase.

GOLSPIE:

ROYAL SUTHERLAND ARMS HOTEL.

BEAUTIFULLY situated within a mile of Dunrobin Castle, the Grounds of which are open to the Public. Free Trout Fishing on Loch Brora for parties staying at the Hotel. Five minutes' walk from sea-shore. Horses and Carriages on Hire. An Omnibus meets Trains. Charges moderate. JAMES MITCHELL, Proprietor.

GREENOCK:

TONTINE HOTEL.

First-Class Family and Commercial

(Nearly Opposite the Caledonian Railway Station),

GREENOCK.

MRS. M'DERMOTT, Proprietrix.

WHITE HART HOTEL,

CATHCART SQUARE.

FAMILY AND COMMERCIAL

Within Three Minutes' Walk of the Railway Stations and Steamboat Wharves.

The Oldest Family and Commercial Hotel in town.

THE ISLAND OF GUERNSEY.

GARDNER'S

ROYAL HOTEL,

FAMILY & COMMERCIAL HOUSE, ESPLANADE, GUERNSEY.

THIS Hotel is situated in the most commanding part of the Island, facing the spacious harbours and the approaches thereto, also having a full front view of the adjacent Islands of Sark, Herm, Jersey, and Alderney. Visitors should be especially careful on landing to ask for the "Royal." *Table d'Hôte.*

JAS. B. GARDNER, *Proprietor.*

GUERNSEY.

OLD GOVERNMENT HOUSE

GARDNER'S PRIVATE HOTEL.

THIS Establishment, being elevated above the town, commands a sea and panoramic view of all the Channel Islands. Visitors should be particular in mentioning the "Old Government House." *Table d'Hôte. Terms on application.*

J. GARDNER, *Proprietor.*

GUERNSEY, CHANNEL ISLANDS.

VICTORIA HOTEL

FAMILY AND COMMERCIAL,

COMMANDS the finest sea-view in the Island. The established reputation of this Hotel is the best guarantee that every attention is paid to the comfort of its Patrons. Hot and Cold Baths always ready.

A Moderate fixed Tariff, including attendance. Private Sitting-Rooms Ladies' Drawing-Room. Table d'Hôte at six oclock. A Porter in attendance on the arrival of Steamers.

M. J. GREEN, *Proprietress.*

HARROGATE WELLS.

BARBER'S GEORGE HOTEL.

VISITORS will find this Hotel conveniently situated, being within three minutes' walk of the Sulphur and Cheltenham Springs, in the immediate vicinity of Public Baths, Concert Rooms, &c., and only seven minutes' walk from the Railway Station. Harrogate being a health resort, it is not expected that the patrons of this Hotel will use Wine, &c., if not required.

TERMS.—Board and Lodgings in Public Room, each 6s. 6d. ; Board and Lodging in Private Rooms, each 7s. 6d. ; Private Sitting Room, 3s. to 5s. ; Attendance and Boots, 1s. 3d. N.B.—Beds charged extra if for less than three nights. Horses' Hay, 10s. 6d. per week. Ostler extra.

The sheltered situation of this Hotel makes it admirably adapted for visitors in spring and autumn. Billiards. Good Stables.

HELENSBURGH.

THE Finest Watering-Place in the West of Scotland. Trains and Boats to Loch Lomond and Trossachs, and Steamer every morning to Dunoon at 8.45, in time to meet the "Iona" for the Highlands by that most celebrated Route—Ardrishaig, Crinan, and Oban, to Staffa and Iona. The alterations and improvements at the QUEEN'S HOTEL are now completed, and the Suites of Apartments for Families cannot be surpassed. The view of the Clyde and Lake is most magnificent. Tourists conveniently arranged. A magnificent Coffee-Room. Smoking and Billiard Room.

All Charges strictly Moderate.

Omnibuses and Carriages to all Steamers and Trains.

A. WILLIAMSON, *Proprietor.*

HELENSBURGH,

IMPERIAL HOTEL,

Newly furnished and decorated.   *Under New Management.*

One Minute's walk from the Railway Station and opposite Steamboat Wharf. All charges strictly moderate.

Tourists for Oban would do well to stay overnight at the "IMPERIAL." Steamer leaves Helensburgh at 8.45 a.m., in connection with "Columba" or "Iona" at Dunoon.

D. SMITH, *Proprietor.*

ILFRACOMBE.

ROYAL CLARENCE
FAMILY AND COMMERCIAL HOTEL.

REPLETE with every Home comfort. A spacious Ladies' Coffee Room, with large number of Bedrooms, has just been added. Large and Spacious Commercial and Stock Rooms. Moderate charges.

First-Class Billiard Room.   Omnibus meets every Train.

R. LAKE, *Proprietor.*

N.B.—General Coach Office and Delivery Agent.

INNELLAN.

ROYAL HOTEL.

JOHN CLARK, in returning thanks to his friends and the Public for past patronage, begs to announce that the new additions to this already large and commodious Hotel are now finished, and include one of the largest and most handsome Dining-Room and Ladies' Drawing Room of any Hotel on the Firth of Clyde, also Parlours with suites of Bed Rooms on each flat.

The Hotel is within three minutes' walk of the Pier, and, being built upon an elevation, commands a sea-view of the surrounding country, including Bute, Arran, the Cumbraes, Ayrshire, Renfrewshire, and Dumbartonshire, making the situation one of the finest in Scotland. The grounds of the Hotel are laid out in walks and interspersed with shrubs and flowers, and are quiet and retired for families. There are also beautiful Drives in the vicinity. The Dining Room has a large Fernery, with water fountain which plays daily during the summer, making it cool and refreshing during the hot weather.

Steamers call at the pier nearly every hour for the Highlands and all parts of the coast. Tourists arriving at the Hotel the night before can have breakfast at Table d'Hôte at 9 A.M., and be in time to join the "Iona" at 10 A.M., for the North, calling at Innellan on her return at 4 P.M.

The Cuisine and Wines are of the finest quality. Large Billiard Room attached. Hot, Cold, and Spray Baths.

Horses and Carriages kept for Hire. Families Boarded by the Day or Week.

INVERARAY.

ARGYLL ARMS HOTEL.

GENTLEMEN staying at the ARGYLL ARMS HOTEL can have excellent SALMON and TROUT FISHING on the Rivers Aray and Douglas, *Free of Charge.*

Ponies kept for ascending Duniquoich Hill.

D. MACPHERSON, *Proprietor.*

INVERARY.

CAIRNDOW HOTEL,
HEAD OF LOCH FYNE.

PARTIES staying at the Hotel can have excellent Salmon and Trout Fishing, free of charge, on the river Kinlass and Loch Restal. The Tarbet, Inverary, and Oban Coaches pass the Hotel daily during the Season.

Horses and Carriages on Hire.

WILLIAM JONES, *Proprietor.*

INVERNESS.

THE ROYAL HOTEL.

Opposite the entrance to the Railway Station.

J. S. CHRISTIE begs to solicit the attention of the travelling Public to this large well-known First-class Hotel, which has been greatly enlarged, and now comprehends, besides extensive First-class Bed Room accommodation, a SPACIOUS and LOFTY LADIES' and GENTLEMEN'S DINING SALOON, with handsome DRAWING ROOM *en suite*, and several elegant and handsomely furnished SUITES of PRIVATE ROOMS; also SMOKING-ROOM, HOT, COLD, and SHOWER BATH ROOMS, etc.

Though immediately *opposite* and within a *few yards* of the Railway Station entrance, the Hotel is entirely removed from the bustle, noise, and other disturbing influences which usually affect the comfort of Hotels situated in close proximity to the Railway.

Table d'Hote daily, and Dinners à la Carte.

The Porters of the Hotel await the arrival of all trains, and an Omnibus attends the Caledonian Canal Steamers. Posting.

ALEXANDER M'LARLANE, Proprietor.

CALEDONIAN HOTEL

UNDER NEW MANAGEMENT.

Two minutes' walk from the Railway Station,

ALEXANDER M'FARLANE begs to intimate he has taken a lease of this well-known first-class Family Hotel, patronised by the Royal Family and most of the nobility of Europe; has recently undergone extensive additions and improvements. Handsomely refurnished throughout.

A LARGE DINING SALOON.

MAGNIFICENT LADIES' DRAWING-ROOM,
OVERLOOKING THE RIVER NESS,

SPACIOUS SMOKING & BILLIARD ROOM (Two Tables),

In point of situation, this hotel is the only one that commands a wide and extensive view of the Ness and the great Glen of "Caledonia."

Table d'Hôte daily.   Dinners à la carte.

AN OMNIBUS ATTENDS ALL THE CANAL STEAMERS.

The Hotel Porters await the arrival of all trains.

POSTING IN ALL ITS BRANCHES

ALEXANDER M'FARLANE, *Proprietor.*

CASS'S HOTEL

(Formerly THE CRAB AND LOBSTER).

VENTNOR, I.W.

THIS Hotel is well established in the seventeenth century of full nowledged the numbers and the requirement of a good Hotel are in the fest for is situated in its own romantic pleasure grounds, in the centre of the far famed Undercliff, whether for pleasure or health, it will be found to be a most agreeable resort.

Apartments en suite for Families.

Coffee Room and Drawing Room for Ladies and Gentlemen.

BILLIARD AND SMOKING ROOM.   HOT AND COLD BATHS.

THE ROYAL HOTEL

(UNDER NEW MANAGEMENT)

STANDS in beautiful grounds and commands fine and amused views. Well sheltered from north and east winds. The Hotel is comfortably furnished, faces due south, and is patronised by first-class families. Every attention and civility shown to visitors. The sanitary arrangements are perfect, and a certificate to this effect has been granted. Conservatory, Billiard Room, Ladies' Drawing Room. Croquet Lawn. Table d'Hote daily.

JERSEY.—STOPFORD HOTEL.

THIS first-class Hotel situated in the best part of St. Heliers, has for up been placed under the management of

BREE'S BOARDING HOUSE.

It has recently been altered, enlarged, and improved, and is now the largest and best-appointed Hotel in St. Heliers.

The Dining Room can accommodate one hundred persons, and is lofty and well ventilated.

The Ladies' Drawing Room is unequalled by any in the Channel Islands.

NEW BILLIARD ROOM AND LAVATORY ON THE GROUND FLOOR.

The Cuisine is perfect, and the Wines excellent.

Table d'Hote every day at Six P.M.

PRIVATE SITTING ROOMS, IF REQUIRED.
Carriages of every description at a moment's notice.

Public and Private Dinners served in the best possible style.

CHARGES MODERATE.

KENMORE

PERTHSHIRE HIGHLANDS.

BREADALBANE HOTEL.

THIS comfortable Hotel is picturesquely situated at the east end of Loch Tay, quite close to Taymouth Castle, the princely seat of the Earl of Breadalbane. From its central position, it forms an admirable point from which to make excursions to the historic and romantic scenes with which the district abounds, while its quiet and retired situation eminently suits it for the invalid and lover of nature. A large and commodious Billiard-room has been added to the Hotel.

Visitors staying at the Hotel are allowed the privilege of fishing for Trout and Salmon in the river Lyon free—and in Loch Tay for a specified charge.

Coaches run daily during the summer months to and from Aberfeldy and Killin, and the Hotel 'Bus awaits the arrival of the principal trains at Aberfeldy. There is a daily post to and from Aberfeldy and Killin.

Letters and Telegrams for Apartments, Conveyances, &c. punctually attended to.

N.B.—The Trout Fishing of Loch Tay, which is free to Parties staying at this Hotel, is considered one of the best in Scotland.

W. MUNRO, Proprietor.

KILLARNEY LAKES.

THE ROYAL VICTORIA HOTEL

Patronised by H.R.H. THE PRINCE OF WALES; by H.R.H. PRINCE ARTHUR; and by the Royal Families of France and Belgium, &c.

THIS Hotel is situated on the Lower Lake, close to the water's edge, within ten minutes' drive of the Railway Station, and a short distance from the far-famed Gap of Dunloe.

TABLE D'HOTE DURING THE SEASON.

There is a Postal Telegraph Office in the Hotel.

Hotel open throughout the year.   Boarding terms from Oct. to June inclusive.

JOHN O'LEARY, Proprietor.

LOCH TAY, PERTHSHIRE.

KILLIN HOTEL.

By Callander and Oban Railway, one of the grandest lines in Scotland for Scenery.

THIS Hotel is situated on the banks of the Lochay, at the head of Loch Tay, amongst some of the finest scenery in Scotland, including Finlarig Castle, the burial-place of the Breadalbane family, Inch Buie, the burial-place of the old Clan M'Nab, and the Falls of Lochay, Auchmore House, Kinnell House, the romantic Glen Lyon, Glenlochay, Glen Dochart, Ben Lawers, and Ben More. Parties Boarded during May and June. Salmon fishing begins 5th February and ends 31st May. Trout fishing Free. Coach runs between Killin, Kenmore, and Aberfeldy, to meet trains north and south from each end.

Posting Establishment complete.

Parties staying at this Hotel can make the tour through the Trossachs and back by Loch Lomond and Glenfalloch in one day.

BUS FROM HOTEL MEETS NORTH AND SOUTH TRAINS.

ALEXANDER STUART, *Proprietor.*

KINGSTOWN.

ROYAL MARINE HOTEL,

KINGSTOWN.

FIRST CLASS FAMILY HOTEL.

Faces Dublin Bay and Kingstown Harbour,

Two minutes from Royal Mail Packet Pier.

FOURTEEN MINUTES FROM DUBLIN BY RAIL.

LUGGAGE PER MAIL SHOULD BE LABELLED "KINGSTOWN."

KILLARNEY LAKE DISTRICT.
THE MUCKROSS HOTEL

COMBINED with strictly moderate charges, contains all that is necessary to promote the comfort and convenience of visitors. It is situated in the most central and beautiful part of the Lake District, and within fifteen minutes' drive of the Railway Station, at which the hotel 'bus attends. Surrounded by pleasant walks and drives, many objects of great interest and beauty, this hotel will be found a most desirable place to spend a few days or weeks.

Angling.—The proprietor has arranged for the use of visitors good private Salmon Fishing. There is also good Salmon and Trout Fishing on the lakes, which are FREE, and anglers can have boats from the proprietor without charge.

Tariff and other particulars on application.

Please be particular to observe the 'bus you enter bears the name, THE MUCK-ROSS HOTEL.

DERWENTWATER HOTEL,
PORTINSCALE, KESWICK.

PATRONISED by H. R. H. Prince Arthur, the Duke of Northumberland, Earl Russell and Family, &c. Tourists and families visiting the Lake District will find the above Hotel fitted on the most modern principles, and every attention paid to their comforts. The Hotel has recently been enlarged.

Large and spacious Coffee-Room, Drawing-Room, and private Sitting-Rooms.

The Hotel stands on the margin of the lake, which it wholly overlooks. It is one mile distant from Keswick. An Angling Association having been formed at Keswick, the lakes and rivers are well protected, and abound in fish. The Wines are of the first quality. Posting, Pleasure Boats, &c. Letters delivered daily. An Omnibus meets every train. Billiard Table by Burroughes and Watts. A Coach every morning at 10 for Buttermere. Mrs. BELL, PROPRIETRESS.

ENGLISH LAKES.
Patronised by H.R.H. the Prince of Wales.
SUN HOTEL
POOLEY BRIDGE, ULLSWATER.

THIS old-established Family Hotel, having been considerably improved, is now replete with every modern accommodation for visitors. From the windows of the Hotel a magnificent view of the lake and mountains is obtained. It is the largest Hotel at the foot of Ullswater, and the only one having a view of the lake. Visitors will find Pooley Bridge a most delightful place of resort, very favourably situated for visiting Haweswater, Lowther Castle, and the neighbouring scenery, not easy of access from any other point. Parties making Pooley Bridge their head-quarters can visit any part of the Lake District and return to the Hotel the same day. The Steamboat plies to the head of the lake three times daily. The Steamer Pier is only four minutes' walk from the Hotel, and Penrith Station six miles, from which coaches run several times daily to Pooley Bridge during the season.

Good Fishing in the Lake and River free to Visitors.
Charges strictly moderate. Posting in all its Branches. Pleasure Boats, Croquet and Lawn Tennis, Billiards, etc. Families boarded by the week on the most reasonable terms.

JOHN BARROW, Proprietor.

CONISHEAD PRIORY

HYDROPATHIC MANSION, NEAR ULVERSTON:

Resident Physician.—Dr. THOMAS MARSHALL (Edin. Univ.)

HOT COLD AND TURKISH SEA AND LAKE WATER BATHS.

Summer Terms, Board and Bath, commencing 1st April, £3 3s. per week.

"THE SCOTSMAN" writes—"Conishead Priory, known far and wide as one of the finest of old English mansions, is now opened to the public as a Hydropathic Establishment. Visitors to the English Lake District will not fail to recall the architectural beauty and enviable situation of the building. The Establishment will be specially welcome to persons who may be in search of healthful relaxation, or of the beautiful in nature. The grounds are, on one side, washed by the waters of the sea, and the house is yet by its happy situation sheltered from the violence of the storm coming either from landwards or seawards. The attraction of the place is enhanced further by the fact, that the Priory is set down at a spot specially convenient for making the tour of the Lakes. The grounds in connection with the Priory extend to 150 acres, about sixteen of which are beautifully laid out in garden and shrubbery; and include excellent croquet and tennis lawns and a bowling-green."

The Guide-Books for the district refer to the Priory as "The Paradise of Furness."

Excursions can be made from the Priory, either by coach or rail, to any part of the English Lake District, returning in the course of the day; and Excursion Parties are arranged on extremely moderate terms.

Lawn Tennis, Croquet, Bowling, and the Scotch Game of Golf, &c.

PROSPECTUS ON APPLICATION TO "THE MANAGER," CONISHEAD PRIORY, NEAR ULVERSTON.

N.B.—The Priory is recommended by high Medical Authority, as a most desirable WINTER Residence. The Directors have completed a new and admirable system of Heating, which is guaranteed to maintain a Summer temperature in the House throughout the boldest months of Winter.

WINDERMERE.

CLOUDSDALE'S CROWN HOTEL.

(Patronised by Royalty, and American Presidents.) A

THE pre-eminence of the CROWN is indicated by the fact that the Hotel has been made a Postal Telegraph Station by Government Authority.

As Head-quarters for Families and Tourists desirous of visiting the other Lakes and Mountain Scenery of this Picturesque District, the CROWN, both by reason of its central situation and convenient access, is acknowledged to be unequalled.

It faces the Lake and Steam Yacht Piers.

The District Coaches run from the CROWN for Ambleside, Grasmere, Keswick; also for Ullswater and Coniston during the Season.

NINETY BEDS.

Table d'Hôte Daily at 6.30 P.M.

OMNIBUSES attend the arrival of Trains at Windermere Station, and Steamers at the Pier.

WINDERMERE.

FERRY HOTEL.

"The most beautiful spot on Windermere is the Ferry."—*Christopher North.*

THIS New and Large Hotel is situated on the Western shore of Windermere, and has most pleasing views of Lake and Mountain. It contains Drawing, Dining, Billiard and Smoking Rooms, etc. The Steam Ferry plies constantly, and Steamers in connection with the Midland and Furness Railways call at the Hotel Pier.

Every description of Pleasure Boats, Carriages, &c.

Bus from the Hotel meets the London and North-Western Trains at the Station.

TARIFF ON APPLICATION TO

BRUCE LOGAN, PROPRIETOR.

WINDERMERE HYDROPATHIC
ESTABLISHMENT

Overlooking "Queen of English Lakes," with magnificent views of mountains and lake.

CHARMING House; elegantly appointed; every comfort and convenience; well ventilated; heated by hot water and open fireplaces. Good table and accomplished *Chef*; moderate terms. The Turkish Bath is PERFECT, with a constant current of hot oxygenised air passing rapidly through it. It can be enjoyed by persons unable to bear the ordinary Turkish baths. Russian, Electro-magnetic, Vapour, and all other baths. Fine Billiard Room with two tables. Resident Physician. Omnibus meets all trains. For prospectus address Manager, Windermere.

D

COMPTON HOTEL

SPACIOUS COFFEE ROOM, with the **LADIES' DRAWING ROOM** adjoining.

CHURCH STREET.

LIVERPOOL.

The Finest COMMERCIAL, BILLIARD, and **SMOKING ROOMS** in the Town.

THIS magnificent building is now the most central Hotel in Liverpool for Families and Visitors, containing 250 rooms, handsomely furnished, with every modern luxury and home comfort. Private Suites of Rooms.

Adjacent to the several Railway Termini and River Landing Stage.

CHARGES STRICTLY MODERATE.

WILLIAM RUSSELL, *Proprietor.*

LIVERPOOL.

SHAFTESBURY HOTEL,

28, 30, and 32 MOUNT PLEASANT, LIVERPOOL.

THREE minutes' walk from Central and Lime Street Stations. Omnibuses from the Landing Stage, the Steamers, and the Exchange, pass every few minutes. Post-Office nearly opposite.

Terms Moderate.

Acknowledged to be one of the best Temperance Hotels in the Kingdom.

LLANDUDNO.

THE IMPERIAL FAMILY HOTEL.

(CENTRE OF BAY.)

IN consequence of the EXTENSIVE PATRONAGE which this Hotel has enjoyed since it was opened in 1872, it has been found necessary to ADD A NEW WING. APARTMENTS *EN SUITE.*

ELEGANT BILLIARD SALOON FOR THREE TABLES.

An Omnibus attends all Trains. EXCELLENT STABLING. *Tariff on Application.*

JOHN CHANTREY, PROPRIETOR.

LLANGOLLEN.

EDWARDS' HAND HOTEL.

THE "HAND,"

Unequalled for the Beauty of its Situation on the Banks of the Dee.

Several Bed-Rooms and Sitting-Rooms have been added to the House to suit the requirements of Families visiting this delightful Neighbourhood.

BILLIARDS.

Omnibuses from this Hotel meet all Trains at Llangollen Station.

LOCH AWE, DALMALLY.

PORT SONACHAN HOTEL

SITUATION unrivalled; views magnificent. Visitors will find this Hotel replete with home-comforts. Messrs. M'Brayne land passengers from the Columba Steamer and from Loch Awe Station (Callander and Oban Railway) at the Hotel Pier.

FISHING ON LOCH AWE FREE. BOATS AND BOATMEN IN ATTENDANCE.

POSTING IN ALL ITS BRANCHES.

Charges strictly moderate.

THOMAS CAMERON, *Proprietor.*

[LOCH EARN HEAD.]

LOCH EARN HEAD HOTEL,

BALQUHIDDER, PERTHSHIRE

10 miles by rail from Callander.

(Under Royal Patronage. Twice visited by the Queen.)

THIS Hotel, which has been long established, has excellent accommodation for Families and Tourists, with every comfort and quiet, lies high and dry, and charmingly sheltered at the foot of the Wild Glen Ogle (the Kyber Pass). It commands fine views of the surrounding Hills and Loch, the old Castle of Glenample, the scenery of the Legend of Montrose, in the neighbourhood of Ben Voirlich, Rob Roy's Grave, Loch Voil, Loch Doine, and Loch Lubnaig, with many fine drives and walks. Posting and Carriages. Boats for Fishing and Rowing free. A 'Bus to and from the Hotel for the Trains during Summer. Coaches to and from Crieff daily in Summer.

R. DAYTON.

The Callander and Oban Railway is now open. Parties breaking the journey here can proceed next morning with greater comfort.

LOCH LOCHLOMOND. LOCH

INVERSNAID HOTEL

THE landing place for Loch Katrine, The Trossachs, Aberfoyle, &c. This Hotel has been considerably enlarged.—The additions comprising Large Dining Rooms, several Bed Rooms, Drawing Room, Billiard Room, &c. All newly furnished.

The scenery surrounding is unsurpassed.

Carriages can be had on hire, and there are also excellent boats and boatmen to be had for the use of Anglers or Excursionists on the Loch.

Arrangements can be made by Parties for Board by the Week or Month.

ROBERT BLAIR, *Proprietor.*

LONDON.
UPPER NORWOOD.
NEAR THE CRYSTAL PALACE.

THE QUEEN'S HOTEL.

THIS unique establishment stands unrivalled for the exquisite picturesqueness and beauty of its situation; its commanding and central position; and the commodiousness and completeness of its general arrangements. Delicate persons, to whom a light bracing air, charming scenery, close vicinity to the Crystal Palace and its amusements, and quiet seclusion, would be an invaluable boon, will find, in this establishment, their wishes fully realised.

"THE QUEEN'S HOTEL, at Upper Norwood, is like a Private Royal Residence, managed with marvellous quietness, and is replete with all domestic comforts and appliances; being a veritable home for individuals as well as families. Lately there have been added some new rooms of magnificent proportions, suitable for balls, wedding breakfasts, public dinners, &c. Ladies and gentlemen can make use of a most delightful coffee room for meals, overlooking the beautiful grounds. For gentlemen there are billiard and smoking rooms, and also a private club. It deserves the special attention of the nobility and gentry, and their families, who may be seeking the means of restoration to health, both of mind and body, without going far from London."—From the *Court Journal.*

SPECIAL NOTICE OF WINTER ARRANGEMENTS AND TERMS AT THE ABOVE HOTEL.

The Patrons of this establishment are respectfully informed that Tourists, Families, and others are received on most reasonable terms for the Winter months—which season has many enjoyments for Visitors at the QUEEN'S HOTEL, owing to its elevated, dry, and salubrious situation, and its convenient vicinity to the Crystal Palace and the Winter Garden, whilst it commands by Rail easy access to the West End, the City, &c.

TABLE GLASS OF ALL KINDS.

GLASS SHADES.
FERN CASES, AQUARIA,
WINDOW CONSERVATORIES,
AND

ORNAMENTAL TILE WINDOW BOXES.

GLASS FLOWER VASES,
Horticultural Glass and Window Glass of all kinds.

PHOTOGRAPHIC GLASS MATERIALS AND APPARATUS.

STAINED AND PAINTED GLASS, FOR MEMORIAL, ECCLESIASTIC, OR DOMESTIC WINDOWS.

GEORGE HOUGHTON AND SON,
89 High Holborn, London.

JAMES BENSON,
Trunk, Portmanteau, and Leather Bag Manufacturer.
LADIES' DRESS TRUNKS, From 7s. 6d.

Waterproof Coats.
Portmanteaus.
Railway Rugs.
Elastic Stockings.
Waterproof Beds.
Driving Aprons.
Overland trunks for India and all parts of the world.
India Rubber Toys
Overshoes, Leggings, &c.

Travelling Bags.
Leather Bags.
Ladies' Bags.
Ladies' Boxes.
Ladies' Dress Imperials.
Waterproof Sheetings.
Ladies' Waterproof Capes.
All kinds of leather Straps.

STRONG AND USEFUL PORTMANTEAUS, From 8s. 6d.

PRICE LIST FREE.

A large number of Second-Hand Travelling Bags, Ladies' Dress Baskets, Portmanteaus, and Trunks.

3, 4, & 263 Tottenham Court Road, & 1 Great Russel Street, London.

GREAT MALVERN.

THE IMPERIAL.

THE attention of Foreign and Home Tourists seeking a salubrious and charming part of England is respectfully drawn to this Establishment, the largest and principal one in the district—comfortable, well appointed, specially adapted for Family Residence, and the charges strictly moderate.

TERMS—FROM £3 : 3s. PER WEEK,

Including Bedroom, Attendance, Meals, and use of Public Rooms.

Special Arrangements made with Families intending to reside for some time.

THE NEW AND ELEGANT SWIMMING BATH,

Part of a complete system of Baths in course of erection—IS NOW OPEN.

Tariffs forwarded on Application.

THE FOLEY ARMS HOTEL

Is situate on the slope of the Hills in the highest part of the town, and from its bay-windows and Terrace the most beautiful views are obtained.

Miss FLIGHT, *Manager.*

EDWARD ARCHER, *Proprietor.*

GREAT MALVERN.

THE ABBEY HOTEL.

AN old established first-class Family Hotel, occupies one of the best positions in Malvern. Is thoroughly well warmed during the colder months of the year. Handsome suites of Apartments. Coffee-Room for Ladies and Gentlemen.

Letters addressed "Manager," insure a reply by first post.

WILLIAM ARCHER, *Proprietor.*

————MANCHESTER.

KNOWSLEY HOTEL,
CHEETHAM HILL ROAD,
Only a few minutes' walk from Victoria Railway Station.

Will be found by Travellers who appreciate Good and Lofty Rooms, and enjoy the Quietude and Comfort which the noisy parts of the City cannot offer, a very acceptable house.

Omnibuses to all parts of the City pass the door every few minutes.

J. B. BRENMEHL, Lessee.

SWAN HOTEL,
MANSFIELD.

UNDER the management of Miss WHITE, daughter of the late Robert White, for 30 years proprietor. The best centre for visiting Sherwood Forest, The "Dukeries," Welbeck, Thoresby, Clumber, Newstead, Hardwick, Bolsover, &c.

"The best plan is to get a carriage from the 'Swan,' at Mansfield."— *Rambles among the Hills*, by Louis J. Jennings.

An Omnibus meets all Trains.

MATLOCK BATH, DERBYSHIRE.
(On the Main Midland Line.)
TYACK'S (LATE IVATTS AND JORDAN)
NEW BATH HOTEL.

THIS first-class old-established Family House, acknowledged to be one of the most homely and comfortable Hotels in the kingdom, is beautifully situated on the highest and most open part of the valley, surrounded by its own extensive pleasure grounds, commanding the finest views of the grand and picturesque scenery for which Matlock Bath (the Switzerland of England) stands unrivalled. Matlock is the most central place for day excursions to the most interesting parts of Derbyshire. A Public Bus to Haddon and Chatsworth daily.

A public Dining Room and Drawing Room. Private Sitting Rooms. Coffee, Smoking, and Billiard Rooms. A large natural tepid Swimming Bath, 68 degrees. TABLE D'HÔTE daily at 6.30 p.m. Excellent Stabling and Coach Houses. Posting, &c.

An Omnibus to and from each Train.
BOOK FOR MATLOCK BATH, NOT TO MATLOCK BRIDGE.
LAWN TENNIS AND CROQUET. GOOD FISHING.

Places of interest in the vicinity:—Buxton, Chatsworth, Haddon Hall, Castleton, Dovedale, Wingfield Manor, Hardwick Hall, &c.

HYDROPATHY.

SMEDLEY'S HYDROPATHIC ESTABLISHMENT,
MATLOCK BRIDGE, DERBYSHIRE.

Physicians { WILLIAM B. HUNTER, M.D., &c. / THOMAS MACCALL, M.D., &c.

THIS Establishment is conducted with the same solicitude and care for the interests of the sick which have characterised it for a period of nearly thirty years, and procured it a high and wide-spread reputation under the late Mr. Smedley. Many additions and improvements have been made, and its usefulness and comfort enhanced. Electric Bells are in every Room—Electric Baths in operation, and there are commodious Billiard and Smoking Rooms.

As a **Winter Residence** this place is admirably adapted for Invalids, especially sufferers from Chest and Digestive disorders, Rheumatism and Gout. It affords warm and well-ventilated Public Rooms, Bedrooms and Corridors, covered Balconies, permitting open-air exercise in all weathers, a handsome and specially-ventilated *Turkish Bath*, and Bath-houses thoroughly reconstructed with all modern improvements. The numbers during the winter months average from one hundred to one hundred and fifty.

Prospectus on application to Manager.

MELROSE.

THE GEORGE AND ABBOTSFORD HOTEL.

THIS Hotel is now enlarged and improved, having Ladies' Drawing-Room, Dining-Rooms, handsomely furnished Suites, 40 Bed-Rooms, Baths (Hot, Cold, and Shower), Billiard Room, and all the necessary appointments of a first-class Hotel, while the charges are the same as those of minor Hotels. Being two minutes' walk from the Railway Station, and the same from the Abbey, the Hotel is the most convenient for Visitors to Melrose. The Proprietors, T. & W. Griffiths (the latter many years with Messrs. Spiers & Pond, and lately their manager for Scotland), have had great experience as Hotel Proprietors and Restaurateurs, and attend personally to all Patrons. Well-appointed carriages, with careful drivers, selected from the large posting establishment of the Hotel, have the sole right of standing in the Station Yard.

The Hotel Omnibus meets all Trains.

MELROSE.

THE ABBEY HOTEL, ABBEY GATE.

THIS is the only Hotel which is built on the Abbey Grounds, at the entrance to the far-famed ruins of Melrose Abbey. An extensive addition having been built to the Establishment, consisting of Private Sitting Rooms, Bedrooms, Billiard-Room, etc. etc., it is now the largest Hotel in Melrose, and only two minutes' walk from the Railway Station.

First-class Horses and Carriages to Abbotsford and Dryburgh Abbey.

An Omnibus attends all trains to convey Visitors' Luggage to and from the Hotel.   GEORGE HAMILTON, PROPRIETOR.

MELROSE, CLEAVER'S KING'S ARMS HOTEL.

Two Minutes' walk from Railway Station and ...

TOURISTS and Visitors coming to this Hotel are cautioned against taking a cab at the Railway Station, and are requested either to take the King's Arms Omnibus (which attends all trains), or walk down to the Hotel, where Carriages of every description can be had for Abbotsford, Dryburgh, etc.

DUMFRIESSHIRE, N.B.

MOFFAT HYDROPATHIC ESTABLISHMENT

AND SANATORIUM,

*Resident Physician—*DR. R. THOMSON FORBES.

THIS Establishment, which occupies a beautiful situation on the western slope of the beautifully wooded Gallow Hill, and within a short distance of the far-famed "Moffat Well," is replete with every comfort for Visitors and Patients. The PUBLIC ROOMS, HALLS, and CORRIDORS are universally recognised as unsurpassed by any similar Establishment, and the BATHS are of the most varied and perfect construction.

MOFFAT has long been a favourite resort for those seeking health and pleasure, and in the Establishment there is the additional attraction of good society and varied amusements.

For full Particulars apply to C. NAU, *Manager.*

MOFFAT SPA.

ANNANDALE ARMS HOTEL.

ROBERT NORRIS, *Proprietor,*

TOURISTS and Visitors to this famous watering-place will find at the Annandale Arms Hotel first-class accommodation, combined with Moderate Charges. Gentlemen will find every attention to their convenience and interests. Omnibuses meet the Trains at Beattock Station. A Summer Excursion Omnibus runs along the route—passing "Craigieburn Wood," Bodesbeck, Grey Mare's Tail, to St. Mary's Loch, every Tuesday, Thursday, and Saturday, in connection with a Coach from Selkirk. Omnibuses ply to the Well every morning. Carriages of all kinds, Job and Post Horses at Hire.

MONMOUTH.

VALLEY OF THE WYE.

THE KING'S HEAD HOTEL
AND POSTING HOUSE.

THIS old-established Hotel, situate in Agincourt Square, the centre of the town, is replete with every accommodation for Families and Tourists, at Moderate Charges.

A SPACIOUS LADIES' COFFEE ROOM.
AND A SUPERIOR BILLIARD ROOM.
An Omnibus meets every Train.

JOHN THOMAS, PROPRIETOR.

OBAN—CRAIG-ARD HOTEL—R. MACLAURIN, *Proprietor.*

TOURISTS and Strangers visiting the West Highlands will find that, whether as regards Situation, Comfort, or Accommodation, combined with Moderate Charges, this elegant Hotel, built expressly for summer Visitors, cannot be surpassed, while it commands an extensive view of the beautiful Bay of Oban and other romantic scenery in the neighbourhood. The Hotel is situated on an elevated plateau near the Steamboat Wharf, to which a new and convenient approach has been lately added. The es and Cuisine are of the first quality. French and German spoken. Table d'Hôte. Apartments may be engaged by the week at a reduced scale.

E

PITLOCHRIE.

FISHER'S HOTEL,

FIRST-CLASS FAMILY HOTEL

AND

POSTING ESTABLISHMENT.

PARTIES wishing to see the magnificent Scenery in this part of the Scottish Highlands will find this Hotel (to which large additions have been made) most convenient, for in One Drive they can visit the

Falls of Tummel, the Queen's View of Loch Tummel;

The Far-Famed Pass of Killiecrankie;

Glen Tilt; The Falls of Bruar, &c.

Pitlochrie is on the direct route to Balmoral Castle, by Spittal of Glen-shee and Braemar; and to Taymouth Castle and Kinloch-Rannoch, by Tummel-Bridge.

Salmon and Trout Fishing on the Rivers Tummel and Garry, and on the Lochs in the neighbourhood.

Job and Post Horses and Carriages of every kind,

By the Day, Week, or Month.

ORDERS BY TELEGRAPH, FOR ROOMS OR CARRIAGES, PUNCTUALLY ATTENDED TO.

PITLOCHRY, PERTHSHIRE.

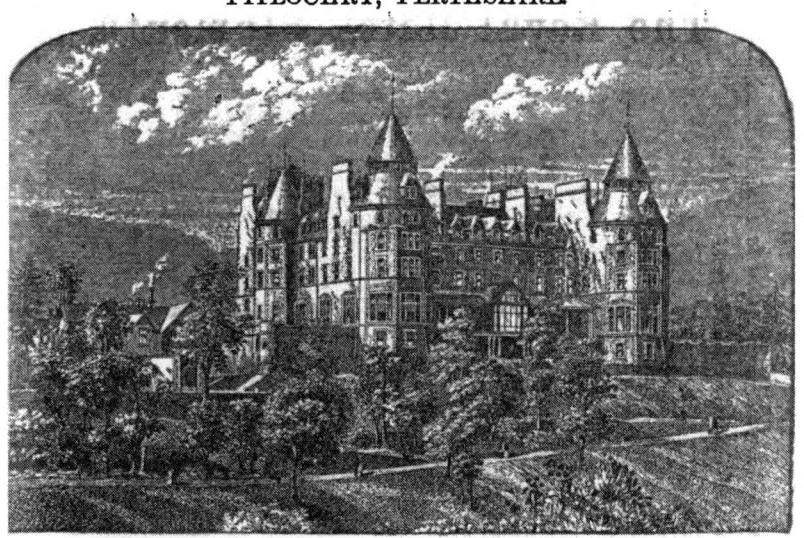

THE ATHOLE HYDROPATHIC ESTABLISHMENT

NO expense has been spared to render this magnificent Establishment complete in all its arrangements. The locality is as widely known for the health-giving qualities of its climate as for the grandeur of its Strath and mountain scenery.

The House occupies a commanding position on the sunny side of Strath Tummel. The Public Rooms are large and richly furnished. The Turkish and other Baths are constructed on the most scientific principles, and for elegance and comfort are not surpassed by any in the country.

The Grounds, extending to 85 acres, abound in natural and artistic beauties, and contain Bowling, Croquet, and Lawn Tennis Greens, Curling Ponds, etc.

The Walks and Drives in the neighbourhood are numerous and inviting. The places of interest within walking or driving distance are—The Pass of Killiecrankie; Lochs Tummel, Tay, and Rannoch; The Falls of Bruar, Tummel, and Moness; Glen Tilt, Blair and Taymouth Castles; Dunkeld, Birnam Hill, Rumbling Bridge, The Birks of Aberfeldy, Black Spout, etc.

A special Telegraph wire connects with the House. Commodious Stable and Coach-house accommodation for Private Carriages.

WILLIAM S. IRVINE, M.D., Consulting Physician.

Prospectuses forwarded on application to ALEX. S. GRANT,

at the Establishment.

The Royal Hotel, Plymouth.

Two Lines of Railway from London and the North of England to Plymouth, viz.,—
London and South-Western and Great Western.

EXTENSIVE POSTING ESTABLISHMENT.

S. PEARSE, PROPRIETOR.

DUKE OF CORNWALL HOTEL,
(Opposite the Railway Station)
POSTAL TELEGRAPH OFFICE.
PLYMOUTH, DEVON.

FIRST-CLASS FAMILY HOTEL
CONTAINING
A HANDSOME GENERAL COFFEE ROOM.
LADIES' DRAWING ROOM.
SMOKING AND READING ROOMS.
LARGE BILLIARD ROOM *(Two Tables).*
SUITES OF APARTMENTS.
HOT AND COLD BATHS.
TABLE D'HOTE DAILY.

Address to the Manager.

ST. LEONARDS-ON-SEA.

ALEXANDRA HOTEL.

THIS HOTEL, situate in the finest position in St. Leonards or Hastings, in the centre of the parade, has been considerably Enlarged and Improved. Fifty more rooms have been added, including a new and spacious Coffee Room, and a large and handsome Reading and Drawing Room. There are elegant suites of apartments, consisting of Bed, Sitting, and Dressing Rooms, French Bedrooms, Excellent Single Rooms, Smoking Room, Bath Room, Gentlemen's Lavatory, and every other convenience.

The Sitting Rooms and French Bedrooms, Coffee Room, and Reading and Drawing Rooms, all face the sea, and in the rear of the premises is a large and tastefully laid out garden.

The Hotel is close to the Pier and Baths, has a complete south aspect directly facing the Sea, and commands an uninterrupted and extensive view of the Channel; it is beautifully appointed, and fitted throughout with every modern appliance conducive to the comfort of visitors. Special arrangements, if desired, are made with families for lengthened periods. Tariff with all particulars will be forwarded on application to   HENRY RADFORD, *Manager.*

SALISBURY.

THE WHITE HART HOTEL.

AN old-established and well-known first-class Family Hotel, nearly opposite Salisbury Cathedral, and within a pleasant drive of Stonehenge. This Hotel is acknowledged to be one of the most comfortable in England.

A Ladies' Coffee Room, a Coffee Room for Gentlemen, and first-class Billiard and Smoking Rooms.

Posting-Masters to Her Majesty. Carriages and Horses of every description.

Tariff on application to H. T. BOWES, *Manager.*

SOUTHSEA, HANTS.
OPPOSITE THE ISLE OF WIGHT.

SOUTHSEA, HANTS.

FIRST-CLASS APARTMENTS, SPLENDIDLY FURNISHED, FACING THE SEA, CLARENCE PARADE. BALMORAL HALL,' 'WELLESLEY HALL,' 'FROGMORE HOUSE.' TRAFALGAR HOUSE. BARRINGTON HOUSE. 6 & 7 DAGMAR TERRACE.

THE healthiest spot in England; commanding an uninterrupted view of SPITHEAD and the ISLE OF WIGHT.

There is a Splendid Esplanade, Magnificent Beach, the best Sea Bathing on the South Coast.

MILITARY BANDS ON THE PIERS DAILY.

A Spacious Common, on which Reviews are frequently held, affording to Visitors a constant source of amusement.

Steam Vessels continually leave the Pier for the Isle of Wight and other places. Assembly Rooms. Libraries. Turkish Baths, etc.

Average Mortality, 14 in 1000.

APPLY TO MANAGERS.

STIRLING.

GOLDEN LION HOTEL.

STUART, LATE CAMPBELL.

THIS Oldest Established and First-Class Hotel is conveniently situated near the Railway Station and Castle. It has been newly renovated and improved, and affords comfortable accommodation to Tourists and Families visiting the Beautiful and Historical Scenery in the vicinity.

Conveyances await the arrival of all Trains and Steamers.

Post Horses and Carriages of every description.

ROBERT STUART, *Proprietor.*

May 1881.

See Shearer's Guide to Stirling and Lakes, 1s. free by Post.
Do.   do.   to Stirling, Maps and Cuts, 6d.

ROSS-SHIRE, N.B.

STRATHPEFFER SPA.

(The Property of the Duchess of Sutherland and Countess of Cromartie.)

STRATHPEFFER (the Harrogate of Scotland) is yearly increasing in popularity, not only on account of the well-known curative powers of its mineral waters (sulphurous and chalybeate), but also because of its being one of the healthiest and most attractive places in the Highlands. Professor (now Sir) Robert Christison of Edinburgh describes the strong well as a pure sulphurous water, and the strongest known in Great Britain. Dr. Murray Thomson, Edinburgh, certified that the Strathpeffer waters deserve a much wider celebrity than they have hitherto enjoyed; that they are invaluable as a curative agent for chronic diseases of the skin, for rheumatism, and gout; and that they act fully on the liver and kidneys, and have their value in many constitutional affections. Dr. Medlock of London writes: "These waters possess several valuable properties which do not belong to any other known sulphur spring."—See Dr. Manson's Guide.

The establishment is in the hands of the Proprietrix, and is placed under the charge of a Manager. There is a resident Medical Practitioner, who has made the waters his special study for several years.

ADDRESS TO THE MANAGER.

THE BEN WYVIS HOTEL,

STRATHPEFFER SPA, ROSS-SHIRE, N.B.

THE HARROGATE OF SCOTLAND.

VISITORS to this popular Watering Place will find this Hotel replete with every comfort combined with charges *strictly moderate*. It stands within its own grounds, which comprise Bowling, Croquet, and Lawn Tennis Greens, is surrounded with grand scenery, and commands a splendid view of Ben Wyvis, the ascent of which can be accomplished from the Hotel in a few hours.

The BEN WYVIS HOTEL. which contains Public and Private Apartments *en suite*, Billiard Room, &c., is within two minutes' walk of the Mineral Wells and Baths, and of Post and Telegraph Offices.

The Hotel is within a mile of the Strathpeffer Station on the Dingwall and Skye Railway, and is a convenient point from which to visit Skye, Loch Maree, Dunrobin, &c. &c.

Orders for Apartments and Carriages punctually attended to.

APPLY TO THE MANAGER. N.B.—POSTING CONDUCTED IN ALL ITS BRANCHES.

SPA HOTEL,
STRATHPEFFER.

MRS. EDWARDS begs to intimate that this Old Established Family Hotel is now open for the Season, where parties can depend on every comfort, combined with moderate charges. The Hotel is beautifully situated, and commands some of the finest views in Strathpeffer.

A conveyance leaves the Hotel three times daily to convey parties to the Pump Room free of Charge.

Posting in all its Branches.

TAYNUILT.

TAYNUILT HOTEL.

THIS Hotel is situated near Loch Etive, within two minutes' walk from the Taynuilt Station on the Callander and Oban Railway. Visitors have the privilege of Salmon and Trout Fishing on the River Awe.

JAMES MURRAY, *Proprietor.*

Post Horses, Carriages, &c.

TENBY.

ROYAL GATE HOUSE HOTEL,

COMMANDING A DELIGHTFUL VIEW OF THE BAY.

(FAMILIES AND GENTLEMEN.)

JOSEPH GREGORY, PROPRIETOR.

THURSO.

HENDERSON'S ROYAL HOTEL.

THIS Hotel has recently been enlarged and expressly fitted up as a First-Class Hotel. The Bedroom and Parlour accommodation are ample, and well adapted to secure the comfort of Commercial Gentlemen and Tourists. Private Parlours and suites of apartments on moderate terms. Daily communication by Steamer to Stromness. Posting in all its departments. 'Bus meets all Trains and Steamers. First-class Billiard Room.

THE TROSSACHS HOTEL,
LOCH KATRINE.
A. BLAIR, PROPRIETOR.

TROSSACHS.

STRONACHLACHAR HOTEL,
HEAD OF LOCH KATRINE.

DONALD FERGUSON begs to intimate that he has lately completed extensive alterations and additions to his Hotel, and that it will be his constant endeavour, as heretofore, to secure every comfort and attention to Tourists and others favouring him with their patronage.

It is the best Fishing Station, and Boats with experienced Boatmen always in readiness.

During the season Coaches run to and from Inversnaid, in connection with Steamers on Loch Katrine and Loch Lomond.

Carriages and other Conveyances kept for Hire.

STRONACHLACHAR, 1881.

YORK.

HARKER'S YORK HOTEL,
ST. HELEN'S SQUARE.

THIS long-established First-Class Hotel occupies the best situation in the City, being nearest to the Minster and the Ruins of St. Mary's Abbey; is free from all noise of Trains, and surrounded by the patent wooden pavement. P. MATTHEWS, *Proprietor;*

Also of the North-Eastern Family Hotel.

GREAT WESTERN RAILWAY.

TOURIST ARRANGEMENTS.

FIRST, SECOND, and THIRD CLASS TOURIST TICKETS, available for two months, and renewable, with exceptions, up to Dec. 31st, are issued during the Summer months of each year, at the principal stations on this Railway, to the Watering and other places of attraction in the WEST OF ENGLAND, including :—

CLEVEDON.	EXETER.	PLYMOUTH.	SCILLY ISLANDS.
WESTON-SUPER-MARE.	DAWLISH.	TRURO.	BRIDPORT.
MINEHEAD.	TEIGNMOUTH.	FALMOUTH.	DORCHESTER.
BARNSTAPLE.	NEWTON ABBOT.	ST. IVES.	WEYMOUTH, & THE
ILFRACOMBE.	TORQUAY.	PENZANCE.	CHANNEL ISLANDS.

To North and South Wales, including—

DOLGELLY.	LLANDUDNO.	CARNARVON.	SWANSEA.
BARMOUTH.	PENMAENMAWR.	HOLYHEAD.	TENBY.
ABERYSTWITH.	BETTWS-Y-COED.	CHEPSTOW.	PEMBROKE.
RHYL.	BANGOR.	TENTERN.	NEW MILFORD.
To BUXTON.	WINDERMERE.	SCOTLAND.	MATLOCK.
ISLE OF MAN.	SCARBOROUGH.	WHITBY.	
To BRIGHTON.	ST. LEONARDS.	ISLE OF WIGHT.	MARGATE.
EASTBOURNE.	HASTINGS.	RAMSGATE.	DOVER.

And to WATERFORD, CORK, LAKES OF KILLARNEY, DUBLIN, ETC.

Passengers holding 1st or 2nd Class Tourist Tickets to the principal stations in the West of England can travel by the 11.45 a.m. Express train from Paddington, which reaches Exeter in *four hours and a quarter*, and Plymouth in *six hours and a quarter*, or by the 3.0 p.m. Express train from Paddington, which reaches Exeter in the same time, and Plymouth in *six hours*.

For particulars of the various Circular Tours, Fares, and other information, see the Company's Tourist Programmes, which can be obtained at the Stations and Booking-offices.

PICNIC AND PLEASURE PARTIES.

From May 2d, 1st, 2nd, and 3rd Class Return Tickets, available for one day only, will be issued (with certain exceptions and limitations) at reduced fares, at all the principal Stations, to parties of not less than six 1st class or ten 2nd or 3rd class passengers.

To obtain these Tickets, application must be made to one of the persons named below not less than three days before, giving full particulars of the proposed excursion.

EXCURSION TRAINS

at low fares will run at intervals during the season, to and from London, Liverpool, Manchester, Birmingham, Bristol, Worcester, Weymouth, West of England, N. and S. Wales, South of Ireland, and all parts of the Great Western system.

Full information as to Trains, Fares, Routes, etc., will be duly announced, and may be obtained on application to the Company's Superintendents :—
Mr. A. Higgins and Mr. W. A. Hart, Paddington ; Mr. J. Gibbs, Reading ; Mr. T. W. Walton, Bristol ; Mr. J. Campfield, Exeter ; Mr. E. C. Compton, Plymouth ; Mr. J. Peach, Penzance ; Mr. G. C. Grover, Hereford ; Mr. J. Kelley, Chester ; Mr. H. Hughes, Birmingham ; Mr. H. Y. Adye, Worcester ; Mr. T. I. Allen, Cardiff ; Mr. H. Besant, Swansea ; and Mr. P. Donaldson, Pontypool Road (Mon.) ; and Mr. C. Boucher, Newport.

Paddington Terminus.　　　　J. GRIERSON, *General Manager.*

F

LONDON & NORTH-WESTERN AND CALEDONIAN RAILWAYS

WEST COAST·ROYAL MAIL ROUTE

BETWEEN

ENGLAND AND SCOTLAND.

1st, 2d, and 3d CLASS TOURIST TICKETS,

Available from the date of issue, up to and including the 31st December 1881, are (during the Season commencing 2d May) issued from all Principal Stations in England to the chief places of interest in Scotland, and also from the same places in Scotland to English Stations.

Passengers by the Through Trains between London (Euston Station) and Scotland are conveyed in

THROUGH CARRIAGES

of the most improved description, and constructed specially for the accommodation of this Traffic.

Saloons, Family Carriages, Reserved Compartments, and all other conveniences necessary to ensure comfort on the journey, can be arranged upon application to Mr. G. P. NEELE, Superintendent of the L. and N.-W. Line, Euston Station, London; the General Superintendent, Caledonian Railway, Glasgow; or to any of the Stationmasters at the Stations on the West Coast Route.

The Passenger Fares, and Horse, Carriage, and Dog Rates between London and Scotland, have been revised and reduced.

By the opening of the line of Railway from CALLANDER to OBAN, direct Railway communication is now afforded by the West Coast Route to Loch Awe, Taynuilt, and Oban.

TABLE OF EXPRESS TRAINS BETWEEN LONDON AND SCOTLAND.

DOWN JOURNEY.

STATIONS.	WEEK DAYS.						SUNDAYS.	
	morn.	morn.	morn.	morn.	night.	night.	night.	night.
London (Euston) dep.	5.15	7.15	10.0	11.0	8.50	9.0	8.50	9.0
Edinburgh (Princes St. Stn.) arr.	4.30	5.50	8.0	9.45	6.45	7.50	6.45	7.50
Glasgow (Central Station) „	4.44	6.0	8.0	10.0	6.55	8.0	6.55	8.0
Greenock . . . . „	5.50	7.15	9.5	11.42	*7.50	*9·40	7.50	9.48
Stirling . . . . „	5.39	..	8.24	10.27	7.21	*8.48	7.21	8.48
Oban . . . . „	..	..	..	4.35	*12.40	..	12.40	..
Perth . . . . „	6.50	..	9.25	11.40	8.15	*9.55	8.15	9.55
Aberdeen . . . . „	10.12	..	..	3.20	12.40	*2.15	12.40	2.15
Inverness . . . . „	..	..	..	8.50	2.45	*6.25	2.45	6.35

No connection from London to Places marked thus (*) on Saturday Nights.

UP JOURNEY.

STATIONS.	WEEK DAYS.						SUNDAYS.	
	aft.	morn.	morn.	morn.	morn.	aft.	morn.	night.
INVERNESS . . dep.	10.0	..	..	..	..	10.18	12.40	10.18	..
Aberdeen . . "	..	..	8.55	9.25	12.30	4.15	12.28	..
	morn.		noon.					
Perth . . . "	8.30	..	12.0	1.55	4.4	7.30	4.4	..
Oban . . . "	..	..	6.0	..	12.0	4.5	..	..
Stirling . . "	9.30	...	1.5	3.24	5.3	8.30	5.3	..
Greenock . . "	9.0	..	1.10	3.0	5.0	8.10	..	..
Glasgow (Central Stn.) . "	10.0	10.4	2.15	4.30	6.0	9.10	6.0	9.10
Edinburgh (Princes St. Stn.) "	10.0	10.35	2.25	4.45	6.10	9.15	6.10	9.15
London (Euston) arr.	8.0	10.40	4.30	5.30	4.5	*8.0	4.5	†8.15
	night.	night.	night.	morn.	morn.	morn.	morn.	morn.

* From Scotland daily, except Sunday.   † From Scotland on Sunday.

THE LIMITED MAIL TRAINS

Travel by this route, and are in connection with the Mail Coaches to the Outlying Districts of the Highlands. These Trains have been accelerated between London and Edinburgh, Glasgow and Perth; and additional accommodation and increased facilities are now afforded to passengers travelling by them.

DAY SALOONS, WITH LAVATORY ACCOMMODATION ATTACHED,

Are run between London and Edinburgh and Glasgow, leaving Euston Station by 10.0 a.m. Down Express, and returning from Edinburgh and Glasgow by 10.0 a.m. Up Express on Week Days. NO EXTRA CHARGE is made for Passengers travelling in these Saloons, and Compartments are specially reserved for Ladies and Family Parties.

SLEEPING SALOONS

Between London and Perth and Glasgow, and CARRIAGES with SLEEPING COMPARTMENTS, are also run between London and Edinburgh and Greenock by the Night Trains. The extra charge for berths in the Saloons or Sleeping Carriages is 5s. in addition to the ordinary 1st class fare.

Passengers are requested to ask for Tickets by the West Coast Route.

Conductors, in charge of the Luggage, &c., travel by the Through Trains.

Dog Boxes specially provided.

Game Consignments conveyed by the Limited Mail.

FAMILY LUGGAGE.—With a view of giving greater facility for the conveyance of heavy Luggage by Passenger Trains, arrangements have been made in all the large towns for carting to the Station, at low rates, the Luggage of Families proceeding to Scotland, and also for forwarding such Luggage by Passenger Trains in advance. The charge for conveyance by Passenger Train is at the rate of 6d. per Truck per Mile, for any weight up to 50 cwts., with a minimum of 10s., and exclusive of a reasonable charge for collection and delivery.

For full particulars of Train Service, Tourist arrangements, &c., see the L. & N. W. and Caledonian Coy.'s Time Books, or West Coast Tourist Guide, which can be obtained at all principal Stations.

April 1881.   *BY ORDER.*

Midland Railway.

The MIDLAND RAILWAY COMPANY provide
SINGLE-HORSE OMNIBUSES

Capable of carrying Six Persons inside and Two outside, with the usual quantity of
Luggage, to meet the Express and other principal Trains at the ST. PANCRAS STATION
when PREVIOUSLY ORDERED.

These Vehicles must be ENGAGED BEFOREHAND, either by written application
to the Station-Master at St. Pancras Station, or by giving notice to the Station-Master
at the starting point (if a Midland Station), or at any Station en route not less than 30
miles from London, so that a telegram may be sent to St. Pancras to have the required
Vehicle in readiness.

The Omnibuses will also be sent to the Hotels or Residences of PARTIES LEAVING
LONDON by MIDLAND RAILWAY, or to the Stations of the Southern Companies at
which passengers may arrive from the Continent on application being made to the Station-Master at St. Pancras, stating the Train by which it is intended to leave St. Pancras.

The charge for the use of an Omnibus will be One Shilling per mile (Driver and a
reasonable quantity of Luggage included), with a minimum charge of Three Shillings.

NEW ROUTE BETWEEN ENGLAND AND SCOTLAND.

THE SETTLE AND CARLISLE RAILWAY is now open for Passenger Traffic, and an entirely
New Service of Express and Fast Trains has been established between the Midland
System and Scotland.

A Morning Express Train runs between London and Edinburgh and Glasgow, in each
direction, with Pullman Drawing-Room Cars attached, and a Night Express Train runs
in each direction between the same places, with Pullman Sleeping Cars attached.
An additional Express Train will run during portions of the months of July, August,
and September, in both directions. First-Class Passengers may avail themselves of the
comfort and convenience of these luxurious Cars on payment of a small charge in addition to the Railway Fare, particulars of which may be ascertained at the Stations.

For the convenience of Passengers to and from the West of England and Scotland,
a New Service of Express Passenger Trains has been established to and from Bristol,
Bath, Gloucester, Cheltenham, Worcester, and Birmingham, in connection with the
Through Service between London and Edinburgh and Glasgow.

The Up and Down Day Express Trains stop half-an-hour at Normanton, in all cases,
to enable Passengers to dine. A spacious and comfortable Dining Room is provided at
that Station for their accommodation.

Through Guards, in charge of the Luggage of Passengers, travel between London
and Edinburgh and Glasgow by the Day and Night Express Trains in both directions.

Passengers by this Route by the Express Trains between London and Edinburgh and
Glasgow are conveyed in Through Carriages of the most improved description, fitted up
with the Westinghouse Continuous Break and all the most approved modern appliances.

Ordinary Return Tickets between Stations in England and Stations in Scotland are
available for the Return Journey on any day within One Calendar Month of the date of
issue.

BELFAST,

BY THE NEW AND SHORT SEA ROUTE via BARROW.

THE capacious New Docks of Barrow, situated within the ancient Harbour of Peel,
under shelter of Walney Island, being now open for traffic, the Swift and Powerful
First-class Paddle Steam Ships "ANTRIM," "ROE," "TALBOT," and "SHELBURNE," will
sail between Barrow and Belfast (weather permitting) in connection with through Trains
on the Midland and Furness Railways; and through Tickets to Belfast, in connection
with the Boat, will be issued now from London, Northampton, Leicester, Nottingham,
Bristol, Birmingham, Derby, Sheffield, Leeds, Bradford, and principal Stations on the
Midland Railway—Return Tickets being available for One Calendar Month.

Passengers to and from London, and other Stations south of Leicester, may break
the journey at Furness Abbey, Leeds, Derby, Trent, or Leicester; and Passengers to
or from Stations west of Derby, at Furness Abbey, Leeds, or Derby, taking care that
from any of those places they proceed by Midland Trains.

TOURISTS' TICKETS.
SCOTLAND.

During the summer months 1st and 3rd Class Tourist Tickets will be issued from London (St. Pancras) and principal Stations on the Midland Railway to Edinburgh, Glasgow, Greenock, Oban, Melrose, Dumfries, Ayr, Stirling, Perth, Dundee, Aberdeen, Inverness, and other places of interest in Scotland.

Saloon, Family, and Invalid Carriages can be obtained for the use of parties travelling to and from Scotland by the Midland Route, by giving a few days' notice to the Stationmaster at any of the principal Stations, or to the Superintendent of the Line, Derby.

MORECAMBE AND THE ENGLISH LAKES.

DURING the Summer months 1st and 3rd Class Tourist Tickets are issued from Principal Stations on the Midland Railway to MORECAMBE, WINDERMERE, AMBLESIDE, GRANGE, FURNESS ABBEY, SEASCALE, PENRITH, KESWICK, and TROUTBECK.

Every Saturday, from May 28th to October 1st, Cheap Excursion Tickets to Morecambe will be issued from Leicester, Nottingham, Derby, Sheffield, Masboro', Barnsley, Normanton, Leeds, Bradford, Keighley, Repton, and principal intermediate points, available to return up to the Tuesday evening after date of issue.

For Fares and further particulars see Tourist Programmes and Special Hand-bills.

MATLOCK AND BUXTON.

First and Third Class Tourist Tickets are issued during the Summer Months from principal Stations on the Midland Railway, and Lines in connection, to Matlock and Buxton.

Passengers holding Tickets to Buxton are allowed to break the journey at principal places of interest on the Line between Matlock and Buxton.

RETURN TICKETS at Low Fares will be issued to MATLOCK and BUXTON, by any of the Through Trains, on Saturdays, from May 28th to October 1st, available for Return by any *Train up to the TUESDAY EVENING after date of issue.*

First and Third Class Tourist Tickets, available for Two Months or longer, are issued during the Summer Months from Principal Stations on the Midland Railway, to

Scarboro', Whitby, Filey, Bridlington, Harrogate, Ilkley, and other Stations in the Yorkshire district.

Yarmouth, Lowestoft, Cromer, Cleethorpes, and other Stations on the East Coast.

Brighton, Hastings, Portsmouth, The Isle of Wight, Bournemouth, and other Stations in the South of England.

Penzance, Plymouth, Torquay, Exeter, Weston-super-Mare, Ilfracombe, and other Stations in the West of England.

Monmouth, Swansea, Tenby, and other Stations in South Wales.

Aberystwith, Llandudno, Rhyl, Bangor, and other Stations in North Wales.

Lytham, Southport, Blackpool, and other Stations on the Lancashire Coast; and to Bath, Malvern, Leamington, Brecon, etc.

For further particulars, see Tourist Programmes and Hand-bills.

Pleasure Parties during the Season, commencing 2d May.

CHEAP RETURN TICKETS

Will be issued to parties of not less than SIX First Class, or TEN Third Class Passengers, desirous of taking Pleasure Excursions to places on or adjacent to this Railway.

For particulars, apply to the Stationmasters on the Line, or to the Superintendent of the Line at Derby.

DERBY, 1881.   JOHN NOBLE, *General Manager.*

CALEDONIAN RAILWAY.

TOURS IN SCOTLAND.

THE CALEDONIAN RAILWAY COMPANY have arranged a system of TOURS—about 70 in number—by Rail, Steamer, and Coach, comprehending almost every place of interest either for scenery or historical associations throughout Scotland, including—

EDINBURGH, GLASGOW, ABERDEEN, DUNDEE, INVERNESS, GREENOCK, PAISLEY, DUMFRIES, PEEBLES, STIRLING, PERTH, CRIEFF, DUNKELD, OBAN, INVERARAY,

The Trosachs, Loch Katrine, Loch Lomond, Loch Earn, Loch Tay, Loch Awe, Caledonian Canal, Glencoe, Iona, Staffa, Skye, Balmoral, Braemar, Arran, Bute, The Firth of Clyde, The Falls of Clyde, &c. &c.

☞ TOURISTS are recommended to procure a copy of the Caledonian Railway Company's "Tourist Guide," which can be had at any of the Company's Stations, and also at the chief Stations on the London and North-Western Railway, and which contains descriptive notices of the Districts embraced in the Tours, Maps, Plans, Bird's-Eye View, &c.

Tickets for these Tours are issued at the Company's Booking Offices at all the large Stations.

The Tourist Season generally extends from JUNE to SEPTEMBER, inclusive.

The Caledonian Co. also issue Tourist Tickets to the Lake District of England, The Isle of Man, Connemara, The Lakes of Killarney, &c.

The Caledonian Railway, in conjunction with the London and North-Western Railway, forms what is known as the

WEST COAST ROUTE

BETWEEN

SCOTLAND AND ENGLAND.

DIRECT TRAINS RUN FROM AND TO

GLASGOW, EDINBURGH, GREENOCK, PAISLEY, STIRLING, OBAN, PERTH, DUNDEE, ABERDEEN, INVERNESS, and other Places in Scotland,

TO AND FROM

LONDON (Euston), BIRMINGHAM, LIVERPOOL, MANCHESTER, LEEDS, BRADFORD, and other Places in England.

Sleeping and Day Saloon Carriages. Through Guards and Conductors.

The Caledonian Company's Trains from and to Edinburgh, Glasgow, Carlisle, &c., connect at Greenock and Wemyss Bay with the "Columba," "Iona," "Lord of the Isles," "Ivanhoe," "Gael," and other steamers to and from Dunoon, Innellan, Rothesay, Largs, Millport, the Kyles of Bute, Arran, Campbeltown, Ardrishaig, Inveraray, Loch Goil, Loch Long, &c. &c.

A full service of Trains is also run from and to Glasgow, to and from Edinburgh, Stirling, Oban, Perth, Dundee, Aberdeen, and the North; and from and to Edinburgh, to and from these places.

For particulars of Trains, Fares, &c., see the Caledonian Railway Co.'s Time Tables.

GENERAL MANAGER'S OFFICE,   JAMES SMITHELLS,
    GLASGOW, 1881.   *General Manager.*

GLASGOW & SOUTH-WESTERN RAILWAY.

DIRECT ROUTE BETWEEN

SCOTLAND & ENGLAND.

THROUGH TRAINS ARE RUN BETWEEN

GLASGOW (St. Enoch) and LONDON (St. Pancras).

Via the GLASGOW & SOUTH-WESTERN and MIDLAND RAILWAYS,

Giving a Direct and Expeditious Service between

GLASGOW, GREENOCK, PAISLEY, AYR, ARDROSSAN, KILMARNOCK, DUMFRIES, &c., AND **LIVERPOOL, MANCHESTER, BRADFORD, LEEDS, SHEFFIELD, BRISTOL, BATH, BIRMINGHAM, LONDON, &c.**

PULLMAN DRAWING-ROOM AND SLEEPING CARS

Are run by the Morning and Evening Trains between GLASGOW and LONDON.

FIRTH OF CLYDE AND WEST HIGHLANDS, VIA GREENOCK.

EXPRESS and FAST TRAINS are run at convenient hours between

GLASGOW AND GREENOCK
(St. Enoch Station)   (Lynedoch St. and Princes Pier Stations)

IN DIRECT CONNECTION WITH THE

"COLUMBA," "IONA," "LORD OF THE ISLES,"

And other Steamers sailing to and from

Kirn, Dunoon, Innellan, Rothesay, Kyles of Bute, Ardrishaig, Oban, Inveraray, Largs, Millport, Kilcreggan, Kilmun, Lochgoilhead, Garelochhead, &c.

Through Carriages are run by certain Trains between GREENOCK (Princes Pier) and EDINBURGH (Waverley), and by the Morning and Evening Express Trains between GREENOCK (Princes Pier) and LONDON (St. Pancras).

RETURN TICKETS issued to COAST TOWNS are available for RETURN AT ANY TIME.

Passengers are landed at Princes Pier Station, from whence there is a Covered Way to the Pier, where the Steamers call; and Passengers' Luggage is conveyed FREE OF CHARGE between the Station and the Steamers.

ARRAN AND AYRSHIRE COAST.

An Express and Fast Train Service is given between GLASGOW (St. Enoch), PAISLEY, and TROON, PRESTWICK, AYR, ARDROSSAN, &c.

From ARDROSSAN the Splendid Saloon Steamer, "BRODICK CASTLE," sails daily to and from the ISLAND OF ARRAN, in connection with the Express Train Service.

Fast Trains provided with Through Carriages are run between STRANRAER, GIRVAN, AYR, &c., and GLASGOW (St. Enoch) and EDINBURGH (Waverley).

IRELAND.

A DAYLIGHT SERVICE is given by the Short Sea Route *via* STRANRAER and LARNE, and a NIGHTLY SERVICE is given by the Royal Mail Steamers *via* GREENOCK, and also by the ARDROSSAN SHIPPING COMPANY'S Full-Powered Steamers *via* ARDROSSAN.

For particulars as to Trains and Steamers see the Company's Time Tables.

APRIL 1881.   W. J. WAINWRIGHT, *General Manager.*

MAENCLOCHOG RAILWAY.

VIEWS FROM THE TOP OF PRICELY MOUNTAIN,

PEMBROKESHIRE,

comprise Coast of Ireland, Coast of Devonshire, Snowdon,
Lundy Island, St. Bride's, Cardigan, and Swansea Bays.

Easy Walk   from

Rosebush   Station,

Vià   *Clynderwen.*

Tourist Season, May 1 to Sept. 30.

Third Class Fare, 1s. there and back.

Range of View, comprising 12 Counties.

1. CARNARVONSHIRE (Wales).		7. CARMARTHEN	(Wales).
2. MERIONETHSHIRE	,,	8. PEMBROKE	,,
3. MONTGOMERY	,,	9. GLAMORGAN	,,
4. CARDIGAN	,,	10. DEVONSHIRE (England).	
5. RADNOR	,,	11. SOMERSETSHIRE (England).	
6. BRECON	,,	12. WEXFORD & WICKLOW (Ireland).	

GREAT SOUTHERN AND WESTERN RAILWAY, IRELAND.

LAKES OF KILLARNEY.

RAILWAY HOTEL

ADJOINS LORD KENMARE'S Demesne, and is situated within easy distance of Ross Castle, Muckross Abbey and Grounds, the Gap of Dunloe, and the principal points of interest.

This Hotel, the largest in the Lake District, possesses unusually good accommodation for Tourists and Families, including spacious and well-furnished Ladies' Drawing Room, Writing, Reception, Billiard, Smoking, Dining, and Private Sitting Rooms. All the Public and Private Sitting Rooms are provided with Pianofortes.

Visitors can arrange to board at the Hotel at charge of £3 13s. per week.

The Porters of the Hotel await the arrival of each Train for the removal of Luggage, &c.

The Manager personally undertakes the formation of Excursion Parties with a view to their comfort and economy.

The Lakes afford excellent Salmon and Trout Fishing.

BOATS, CARRIAGES, PONIES, &c., WITH STEADY ATTENDANTS, ALWAYS READY FOR ENGAGEMENT.

Boatmen, Guides, Drivers, and other Servants of the Hotel, are paid ample wages, and are not permitted to solicit Visitors for Gratuities.

A Wagonette will run, from 1st June to 30th September, between the Hotel and Ross Castle. Fare, 6d. each way.

From 1st MAY to 31st OCTOBER 1881,

TOURISTS' TICKETS from

DUBLIN TO KILLARNEY AND BACK

Will be issued by the Trains which run direct to Killarney, at the following Fares, viz.—

		FIRST CLASS.	SECOND CLASS.
Single Ticket for One Passenger	.	£2 10 0	£2 0 0
Do.	Two Passengers	4 10 0	3 12 0
Do.	Three ,,	6 7 6	5 2 0
Do.	Four ,, .	8 0 0	6 8 0
Do.	Five ,, .	9 7 6	7 10 0
Do.	Six ,, .	10 10 0	8 8 0
Do.	Seven ,, .	11 7 6	9 2 0
Do.	Eight ,, .	12 0 0	9 12 0

AVAILABLE FOR RETURN ON ANY DAY

WITHIN ONE CALENDAR MONTH.

The time of these Tickets can be extended upon the terms stated in the Company's Tourist Programme.

N.B.—Tickets to KILLARNEY can be obtained at the principal Stations on the London and North Western, Midland Great Western, Lancashire and Yorkshire, Manchester, Sheffield, and Lincolnshire, North Staffordshire, Caledonian, and North British Railways, and Railways in Ireland.

KINGSBRIDGE, DUBLIN, 1881.

FLEETWOOD TO BELFAST

AND THE

NORTH OF IRELAND.

EVERY EVENING (SUNDAYS EXCEPTED).

In connection with the Lancashire and Yorkshire, and London and North-Western Railways.

THE NORTH LANCASHIRE STEAM NAVIGATION COMPANY'S Royal Mail Steam Ships,

EARL OF ULSTER (New Steamer), | THOMAS DUGDALE,
DUKE OF CONNAUGHT, • | PRINCESS OF WALES,

LEAVE FLEETWOOD FOR BELFAST

Every Evening (Sundays excepted), at or after 7.40 p.m., after arrival of trains from London, Birmingham, Hull, Newcastle, Bradford, Leeds, Liverpool, Manchester, Preston, and all parts of the Kingdom ; returning

FROM BELFAST TO FLEETWOOD

Every Evening (Sundays excepted), at 8.0 p.m., arriving in Fleetwood in time for early morning trains to the above places.

FARES.—SALOON, 12s. 6d. ; STEERAGE, 5s. ; RETURN TICKETS (available for one month), SALOON, 21s. ; STEERAGE, 8s. 6d. Through Tickets (single and return) are also issued from all the principal Stations of the London and North-Western, Lancashire and Yorkshire, North-Eastern, Great Western, Great Northern and Manchester, Sheffield, and Lincolnshire Railway Companies, to Belfast, and *vice versa.*

SPECIAL TOURISTS' TICKETS AVAILABLE FOR TWO MONTHS

are issued during the Summer Season, *via* the Fleetwood Route, whereby Tourists may visit all places of interest in the North of Ireland and Dublin. For particulars, see the Lancashire and Yorkshire and London and North-Western Companies' Books of Tourists' Arrangements.

At Fleetwood the railway trains run alongside the steamers, and passengers' luggage is carried from the train at the quay on board FREE OF CHARGE.

Fleetwood is unrivalled as a steam packet station for the North of Ireland, and the unexampled regularity with which the Belfast Line of Steamers have made the passage between the two ports for more than thirty years, is probably without a parallel in steamboat service, and has made this Route the most popular, as it is certainly the most Expeditious and Desirable, for Passengers, Goods, and Merchandise, between the great centres of commerce in England, and the North and North-West of Ireland.

For further information, see Bradshaw's Guide, page 351, or apply at any of the stations of the Railway Companies before named ; T. C. HAINES, 20 Donegall Quay, Belfast ; or to THOS. H. CARR, FLEETWOOD.

'ANCHOR LINE.'
DIRECT STEAM COMMUNICATION
(Carrying the United States' Mails)
By the First-Class Powerful Steam Packet Ships,

ACADIA	CALEDONIA	FURNESSIA	OLYMPIA
ALEXANDRIA	CALIFORNIA	GALATIA	ROUMANIA
ALSATIA	CASTALIA	HESPERIA	SCANDINAVIA
ANCHORIA	CIRCASSIA	HISPANIA	SCOTIA
ARMENIA	COLUMBIA	INDIA	SIDONIAN
ASSYRIA	DEVONIA	ISCHIA	TRINACRIA
AUSTRALIA	DORIAN	ITALIA	TYRIAN
BELGRAVIA	ELYSIA	JUSTITIA	UTOPIA
BOLIVIA	ETHIOPIA	MACEDONIA	VICTORIA
BRITANNIA			

GLASGOW TO NEW YORK,
Via LONDONDERRY (MOVILLE, LOCH FOYLE).
Carrying U.S. Mails, every Thursday ; and from NEW YORK, Pier 20,
N. River, every Saturday.
SALOON PASSAGE, £12 : 12s., £14 : 14s., and £16 : 16s. SECOND CABIN,
£8 : 8s. STEERAGE, £6 : 6s.

TO AND FROM LONDON AND NEW YORK,
Direct, every Saturday.
SALOON PASSAGE, £10 : 10s. to £15 : 15s. STEERAGE, £6 : 6s.

GLASGOW TO BOMBAY,
Via LIVERPOOL AND SUEZ CANAL, every Fortnight.
SALOON PASSAGE, Fifty Guineas from Liverpool.

GLASGOW AND MEDITERRANEAN SERVICE.
Lisbon, Gibraltar, Genoa, Naples, Messina, Palermo, and
other Ports as required. And from thence to New York,
Every Fortnight.
Glasgow to Lisbon, £6 : 6s. ; Gibraltar, £8 : 8s. ; Genoa, £12 : 12s. ;
Leghorn, £13 : 13s. ; Naples, £14 : 14s. ; Messina or Palermo, £16 : 16s.
Round Voyage and back to Glasgow, 35 Guineas.

Passengers Booked to all parts of the
United States and Canada.
Apply to HENDERSON BROTHERS, 18 Leadenhall Street, London ; 17
Water Street, Liverpool ; 1 Panmure Street, Dundee ; Foyle Street,
Londonderry ; 2 Rue Noallis, Marseilles ; 8 Rue Scribe, Paris ; 7 Bowling
Green, New York ; or to
HENDERSON BROTHERS,
47 Union Street, Glasgow.

TO TOURISTS.

STEAM TO CAITHNESS

AND THE

ISLANDS OF ORKNEY AND SHETLAND.

THE swift and elegant Steamships "St. Magnus," "St. Nicholas," "St. Clair," and "Queen" (*carrying H.M. Zetland Mails*) sail from Albert Dock, Leith, and Aberdeen during summer, to Thurso once a week, and to Wick, Kirkwall, and Lerwick twice a week. Fares very low, and Passenger accommodation first-class.

** The new Steamship "Earl of Zetland," built and specially adapted for the trade, sails twice a week between Lerwick and the North Isles of Shetland; and the S.S. "Orcadia," sails between Kirkwall and the Islands of Orkney, giving Tourists unequalled facilities for visiting the Islands with every comfort.

Apply to CHARLES MERRYLEES, Manager, Aberdeen; or to GEORGE HOURSTON, Agent, 64 Constitution Street, Leith, and 18 Waterloo Place, Edinburgh.

NEW ROUTE.

GLASGOW AND THE HIGHLANDS.

THE Steamers "Dunara Castle" and "Aros Castle" sail from Glasgow for Oban, Colonsay, and Iona, Aros, Tobermory, Croag, and Bunessan (Mull), Tyree, and Coll, Struan, Carbost, Dunvegan, Stein, and Uig (Skye), Tarbert and Rodel (Harris), Lochmaddy, Kallin, Carnan and Lochboisdale (Uist), and Barra.

** The Tourist who desires (within the limits of a week, and at a reasonable expense) a panoramic view of the general scenery of the Hebrides, with all its varied beauty, sublimity, and grandeur, has no better opportunity afforded him than by taking the round in one of these Steamers.

Further information and Time-bills may be had by applying to
MARTIN ORME, 20 Robertson Street, Glasgow.

GLASGOW, BELFAST, BRISTOL, CARDIFF, AND SWANSEA.

Carrying Goods for Newport, Exeter, Gloucester, Cheltenham, etc.

The Screw Steamships
AVON, SOLWAY, SEVERN, PRINCESS ALEXANDRA,
or other Vessels,
Are intended to Sail as under :—

GLASGOW to BRISTOL and SWANSEA—Every Monday, at 2 P.M.
GLASGOW to BRISTOL and CARDIFF—Every Friday, at 2 P.M.
BELFAST to BRISTOL and SWANSEA—Every Tuesday.
BELFAST to BRISTOL and CARDIFF—Every Saturday.
BRISTOL to BELFAST and GLASGOW—Every Wednesday and Friday.
SWANSEA to BELFAST and GLASGOW—Every Saturday.
CARDIFF to BELFAST and GLASGOW via BRISTOL—Every Monday.
FARES from GLASGOW—Cabin, 20s.; Steerage 12s. 6d.; Soldiers and Sailors, 10s.
   ,,   from BELFAST—Cabin, 17s. 6d.; Steerage, 10s.
RETURNS for Cabin and Steerage at Fare and a half, available for Two MONTHS.
These Steamers have splendid Cabin accommodation for passengers.

For Rates of Freight and further particulars, apply to

WILLIAM SLOAN & CO., 140 Hope Street, Glasgow.

ABERDEEN
AND
LONDON

Average Passage
36 Hours.

THE ABERDEEN STEAM NAVIGATION COMPANY'S STEAMSHIPS

BAN-RIGH, CITY OF LONDON, or CITY OF ABERDEEN,
will be despatched (weather, etc., permitting) from ABERDEEN, and from The Aberdeen Steam Navigation Co.'s Wharf, Limehouse, LONDON, every Wednesday and Saturday.

FARES—including Stewards' Fees—*Private Cabins* accommodating four passengers, £6. *Private Cabins*, if occupied by fewer than four passengers, £5.

Single Tickets—First Cabin, 30s. ; Second Cabin, 15s. ; Children under fourteen years, 15s. and 10s. *Return Tickets*—available for three months—45s. and 25s. ; Children, 25s. and 15s.

Passengers will please observe that during the season the Co.'s steamer 'Ich Dien' will start from the Temple Pier, Thames Embankment, one hour before the advertised times of sailing, conveying passengers and their luggage alongside the Aberdeen Steamers free of charge. Porters in the Company's service will assist with the luggage.

For further particulars apply to JOHN A. CLINKSKILL, Agent, The Aberdeen Steam Navigation Co.'s Wharf, Limehouse ; and 102 Queen Victoria Street, E.C., London ; or to CHARLES SHEPHERD, Manager, Waterloo Quay, Aberdeen.

LEITH AND LONDON

THE LONDON & EDINBURGH SHIPPING COMPANY'S
SPLENDID FAST-SAILING SCREW-STEAMSHIPS
MALVINA (New Steamer),

MARMION, IONA, MORNA, OR OTHER OF THE COMPANY'S STEAMERS,

Sail from VICTORIA DOCK, LEITH, every *Wednesday* and *Saturday* after-
noon ; and from HERMITAGE STEAM WHARF, LONDON, every *Wednesday* and *Saturday* morning.

For Rates of Freight and Fares, apply to THOMAS AITKEN,
8 Commercial Street, Leith.

GOLD MEDAL, PARIS.
12th INTERNATIONAL MEDAL AWARDED.
First Award for Chocolate and Cocoa at the Sydney Exhibition.

FRY'S COCOA

FRY'S COCOA EXTRACT,
GUARANTEED PURE COCOA ONLY.
A perfectly Pure and Delicious Beverage, prepared exclusively from Choice Cocoa Nibs (deprived of the superfluous oil).

" If properly prepared, there is no nicer or more wholesome preparation
of Cocoa."—*Food, Water, and Air*, DR. HASSALL.

" Strictly pure, and well manufactured in every way."—W. W. STOD-
DART, F.I.C., F.C.S., *City and County Analyst, Bristol.*

"Pure Cocoa, from which a portion of its oily ingredients has been
extracted."—CHAS. A. CAMERON, M.D., F.R.C.S.I., *Analyst for Dublin.*

J. S. FRY AND SONS, BRISTOL AND LONDON.

DUBLIN & GLASGOW STEAM PACKET COMPANY.

THE Company's splendid Saloon Paddle Steamships--DUKE of ARGYLL, DUKE of LEIN-STER, LORD CLYDE, LORD GOUGH, or other Steamers, are intended to Sail, unless prevented by any unforeseen occurrence, to and from GLASGOW & DUBLIN, calling at GREENOCK.

SAILINGS.

GLASGOW to DUBLIN.—Every Monday, Wednesday, and Friday, and every alternate Tuesday, Thursday, and Saturday.

DUBLIN to GLASGOW.—Every Monday, Wednesday, and Friday, and every alternate Tuesday, Thursday, and Saturday. Train from Central Station, Glasgow, at 6.30 p.m.; Steamer leaving Greenock about 7.30 p.m.

Fares.—From Glasgow (including Steward's Fees), Cabin 15s.; Ditto (including Rail to Greenock), 16s. 3d. Return Tickets (available for Six Months), £1:2:6; Ditto (including Rail to Greenock), £1:5s. Steerage fare from Glasgow, 6s. (including rail to Greenock), 6s. 9d. Return Tickets (available for six months), 10s. (including rail to Greenock), 11s. 6d. Through Express Train (per Caledonian Railway) from Leith at 4.30 p.m., and from Edinburgh (Princes Street Station) at 5 p.m. to Greenock in direct connection with the Dublin Steamer. Passengers are also booked through from the following Railway Stations to Dublin, and *vice versa,* viz.—

	Single.		Return, available for 2 mths.			Single.		Return, available for 2 mths.	
	1st cl.	3 cl. & Strage.	1st cl.	3 cl. & Strage.		1st cl.	3 cl. & Strage.	1st cl.	3 cl. & Strage.
	s. d.	s. d.	s. d.	s. d.		s. d.	s. d.	s. d.	s. d.
Alloa	19 1	8 7	26 4	13 2	Forfar	30 0	13 10	40 9	19 10
Arbroath	30 8	14 3½	40 10	20 5	Hamilton	17 3	7 4	27 0	12 9
Aberdeen	39 6	18 8	51 11	25 10	Inverness	48 6	23 3	73 2	..
Crieff	23 6	10 7½	31 11	15 10	Leith	20 0	8 6	30 0	14 0
Callander	21 0	9 9	28 9	14 8	Montrose	33 6	15 8	44 5	22 1
Dundee (W.)	26 0	12 1½	31 6	18 4	Perth	24 6	11 3	33 2	16 6
Dumfries	22 9	12 1½	41 11	21 5	Paisley	16 3	6 3	25 0	11 6
Edinburgh	20 0	8 6	30 0	14 0	Stirling	19 0	8 5	26 3	13 0

Booking Office at Dublin for Passengers—1 EDEN QUAY. Chief Office and Stores—71 NORTH WALL, DUBLIN. Goods carried at Through Rates from Glasgow and Greenock to Inland Towns in Ireland; and also from a number of the Principal Railway Stations in Scotland to Dublin, and Inland Stations in Ireland, and *vice versa.* Further particulars, monthly Bills, &c., on application to the undermentioned agents:—

JAMES LITTLE & CO., Excise Buildings, Greenock, and

HENRY LAMONT, 93 Hope Street, adjoining Central Station; and Broomielaw, Glasgow.

A. TAYLOR, Dublin, Secretary. E. MANN, Dublin, General Manager.

BLACK'S
Large Map of Scotland
IN TWELVE SHEETS.
SCALE—4 MILES TO THE INCH.

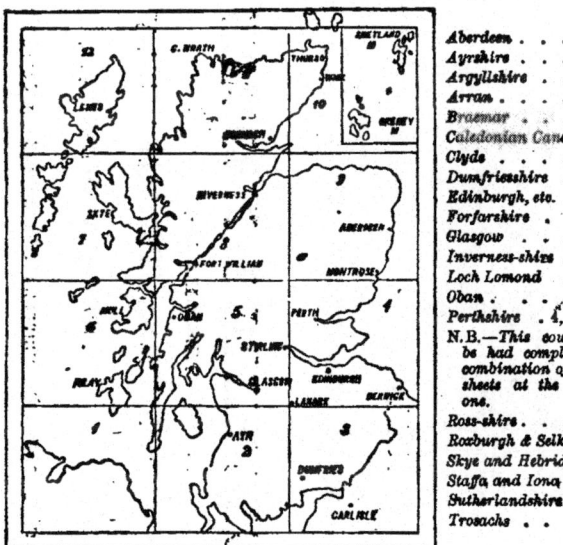

	Sheet No.
Aberdeen	9
Ayrshire	2
Argyllshire . . .	5
Arran	2
Braemar	9
Caledonian Canal .	8
Clyde	5
Dumfriesshire . .	3
Edinburgh, etc. . .	4
Forfarshire . .	4, 9
Glasgow . . .	5
Inverness-shire .	8, 11
Loch Lomond . .	5
Oban	5
Perthshire . 4, 5, 8, 9	

N.B.—This county may be had complete by a combination of the four sheets at the price of one.

Ross-shire . . .	8
Roxburgh & Selkirk	3
Skye and Hebrides .	7
Staffa and Iona . .	6
Sutherlandshire .	11
Trosachs	5

Separate Sheets, in Cases, 2s. 6d.

Set of twelve sheets, in Book Case . . .	£1	1	0
Ditto mounted on Cloth, and in Book Case	1	8	0
Ditto do. in two large Sheets, do.	1	11	7
Ditto do. on Rollers, Varnished .	2	2	0
Perthshire complete	0	2	6

EDINBURGH : ADAM AND CHARLES BLACK.

G

ENCYCLOPÆDIA BRITANNICA

Ninth Edition.

EDITED BY PROFESSOR THOS. SPENCER BAYNES, LL.D.

ASSISTED BY UPWARDS OF 600 CONTRIBUTORS.

Illustrated with Maps and numerous Engravings on Wood and Steel.

THIS Edition of the ENCYCLOPÆDIA BRITANNICA is designed to be completed in about twenty-one volumes, and these will be issued at the rate of two or three volumes a year, as circumstances will permit. Vols. I to XII. are now published, and Vol. XIII. is in the press. "This volume (XII.) brings the work down to the article Indus, and all the articles, large and small, seem to be done with the same conscientious care and thoroughness which have characterised previous volumes."—*Times*, April 18, 1881.

Price per Volume, in Cloth, 30s.; half Russia, 36s.

A detailed Prospectus, with names of Contributors, and specimen pages, may be obtained on application to any Bookseller, or will be forwarded by the Publishers.

EDINBURGH: ADAM AND CHARLES BLACK.

NEW WORK ON GARDENING.

In Crown 8vo, Price 6s. 6d.

E P I T O M E

OF

GARDENING

By THOMAS MOORE, F.L.S.
AND Dr. M. F. MASTERS, F.R.S.

JOINT EDITORS OF THE 'GARDENER'S CHRONICLE.'

Illustrated with upwards of 200 Woodcuts.

CONTENTS.

1. PRINCIPLES OF HORTICULTURE.
2. THE GARDEN.
3. STRUCTURE AND APPLIANCES.
4. OPERATIONS.
5. FLOWERS,
6. TREES AND PLANTS.
7. FRUITS.
8. VEGETABLES.
9. CALENDAR.
10. INDEX.

"To every amateur this book should be a boon, and we feel sure it will soon find a place on the bookshelves of every one interested in gardening; and from its convenient size will be in constant use for reference."—*Midland Counties Herald.*

EDINBURGH: ADAM & CHARLES BLACK.

THE WAVERLEY NOVELS.

AUTHOR'S EDITIONS.

COMPLETE SETS at the following Prices:—

1. Price £1 : 1s. **Sixpenny Edition** in 4 vols. 8vo, half French morocco. The same in half calf, price £1 : 7s.

2. Price £1 : 13s. **Shilling Edition,** Illustrated with 125 Wood Engravings, in 12 vols. fcap. 8vo, cloth. The same in leather back, extra gilt, price £2 ; or in half calf, price £2 : 12s.

3. Price £1 : 17s. **Pocket Edition,** Illustrated with a Steel Portrait and Woodcut Vignettes, in 25 vols. 12mo, cloth. The same in limp Cape morocco, price £3 : 5s.

4. Price £4 : 4s. **Centenary Edition,** with Additional Notes, Illustrated with Woodcut Frontispieces and Vignettes, in 25 vols. crown 8vo, cloth. The same may be had in half calf or morocco.

5. Price £7 : 4s. **Author's Favourite Edition** (1847), with Steel Frontispieces and Woodcut Vignettes, in 48 vols. fcap. 8vo, cloth.

6. Price £7 : 7s. **Illustrated Edition,** with 1600 Woodcuts and 96 Steel Plates, in 48 vols. fcap. 8vo, cloth.

7. Price £10 : 12 : 6. **New Library Edition,** Illustrated with about 200 Steel Engravings by the most Eminent Artists of their time, and printed in large type, in 25 vols. large 8vo, cloth.

EDINBURGH : A. & C. BLACK.

W. H. SMITH AND SON'S
REDUCED ORDNANCE MAPS,
For Travellers and Tourists.

"These splendid Maps, unquestionably the most perfect ever published, have been compiled from the Ordnance and Admiralty Surveys, with railways up to the latest date. Their particulars are most minute and accurate; every possible information that a Map can give is afforded."—*Liverpool Albion.*

PRICE 1s. EACH,
Full Coloured, Cloth Cases. Scale, Four Miles to an Inch.

ALDERSHOT, showing Surrey, Hampshire.
———— Camp and excursions; scale 2 inches to a mile.
BEDFORD, Huntingdon, Northampton, etc.
BIRMINGHAM, showing Wolverhampton, Coventry, Leamington.
———— PLAN OF THE TOWN.
BRIGHTON, showing Hastings, Chichester.
———— PLAN OF TOWN AND SUBURBS.
BRISTOL, showing Bath, Bridgewater.
BRITISH ISLES, RAILWAY MAP OF.
———— on linen, 2s.
CAMBRIDGE, showing Ely, Bury St. Edmunds, etc.
CARLISLE, showing Silloth, Maryport, Cockermouth, etc.
CARMARTHEN & SOUTH-WEST WALES.
CHESHIRE, showing the Potteries, Manchester, Wigan, etc.
CORNWALL, showing Land's End.
DERBY, showing Buxton, Sheffield, etc.
DEVON, NORTH, Barnstaple, Bideford, etc.
———— SOUTH, and Dartmoor.
DORSETSHIRE, showing the New Forest, Salisbury, Yeovil, etc.
EASTBOURNE, PLAN OF.
ESSEX, COUNTY MAP.
EXETER, showing Torquay, Plymouth.
GLOUCESTER, showing Cheltenham.
HASTINGS AND ST. LEONARDS, PLAN OF.
HEREFORD, showing Malvern, the Wye.
HERTFORD.
IPSWICH, Colchester, Newmarket, etc.
ISLE OF WIGHT and part of Hants.
———— 1 inch to a mile.
KENT, Gravesend, Margate, Ramsgate, Dover, Folkstone, etc.
LAKE DISTRICT OF WESTMORELAND AND CUMBERLAND.
———— Ulverston and Furness, scale 1 inch to a mile.
LANCASHIRE COUNTY.
LAND'S END AND CORNWALL.
LEICESTER, Lichfield, Stamford, etc.
LINCOLN, showing Boston, Gainsborough, Grimsby, etc.
LIVERPOOL, showing Southport, Wigan, Warrington, Crewe, Chester, etc.
———— PLAN OF THE CITY.

LEEDS, showing Bradford, Wakefield, Halifax, York, Doncaster, etc.
LONDON, showing Windsor, Guildford, Maidstone, Southend, etc.
LONDON, PLAN of, 1s. on paper, and 2s. on linen.
———— ENVIRONS OF. Scale one inch to a mile (and on linen 2s.)
MANCHESTER, Buxton, Macclesfield, Blackburn, Southport, etc.
———— PLAN OF THE CITY.
MIDDLESEX COUNTY.
NEWCASTLE, Durham, Sunderland, Hartlepool, Morpeth, etc.
NEWPORT, MONMOUTH, showing Lower Wye, Cardiff, Merthyr Tydvil, etc.
NORFOLK COUNTY.
NORTHUMBERLAND, County of.
NORWICH, showing Yarmouth, Lowestoft.
NOTTINGHAM, Derby, Lincoln, Leicester.
OXFORD, Reading, Banbury.
PETERBOROUGH, showing Huntingdon, Grantham, Melton-Mowbray, etc.
PLYMOUTH, showing Dartmoor, Cornwall.
———— PLAN OF THE TOWN.
PRESTON, showing Lancaster, Wigan, Rochdale, Blackpool, etc.
RUGBY, showing Leamington, Warwick, Coventry, Stratford-on-Avon.
SALISBURY, Isle of Wight, Southampton, Portsmouth, Dorchester, etc.
SCARBOROUGH and Yorkshire Coast, showing York, Whitby, etc.
SCOTLAND, TOURIST'S MAP, and on linen, 2s.
SHREWSBURY, Welshpool, Stafford.
SOMERSETSHIRE, River Severn.
THAMES, THE RIVER.
TUNBRIDGE, showing Rochester, Maidstone, Lewes, etc.
WALES, North, showing Anglesea, Carnarvon, Denbigh, Merioneth.
———— CENTRAL, showing Dolgelly, Aberystwith, Montgomery, etc.
———— SOUTH-WEST, showing Carmarthen, Pembroke, Cardigan.
———— SOUTH-EAST, showing Monmouth, Brecknock, Glamorgan.
YORKSHIRE, COUNTY MAP.

London: W. H. SMITH & SON, 186 Strand, & at the Railway Bookstalls.

BIRMINGHAM.

MESSENGER & SONS,

MANUFACTURERS OF

CHANDELIERS, CANDELABRA AND GAS FITTINGS,

IN BRONZE AND ORMOLU:

Carefully constructed on a principle to avoid the Escape and Odour of Gas.

MESSENGER AND SONS' CASE IN THE INTERNATIONAL EXHIBITION.

MEDAL AWARDED.

REPORT OF THE JURORS :—"Messenger and Sons, for great progress, and also for Elegance of Design and Excellent Workmanship."

IRON RAILINGS FOR STAIRCASES, BALCONIES, &c.;

Also, Manufacturers and Patentees of

RAILWAY SIGNAL, CARRIAGE ROOF, AND OTHER LAMPS AND CARRIAGE FURNITURE.

Dr. J. COLLIS BROWNE'S
CHLORODYNE.

THE ORIGINAL AND ONLY GENUINE.

CHLORODYNE is the best remedy known for COUGHS, CONSUMPTION, BRONCHITIS, ASTHMA.

CHLORODYNE effectually checks and arrests those too often fatal diseases known as DIPHTHERIA, FEVER, CROUP, AGUE.

CHLORODYNE acts like a charm in DIARRHŒA, and is the only specific in CHOLERA and DYSENTERY.

CHLORODYNE effectually cuts short all attacks of EPILEPSY, HYSTERIA, PALPITATION, and SPASMS.

CHLORODYNE is the only palliative in NEURALGIA, RHEUMATISM, GOUT, CANCER, TOOTHACHE, MENINGITIS, &c.

The Right Hon. EARL RUSSELL has graciously favoured J. T. DAVENPORT with the following :—
"Earl Russell communicated to the College of Physicians that he received a despatch from Her Majesty's Consul at Manilla, to the effect that Cholera has been raging fearfully, and that the only remedy of any service was CHLORODYNE."—See *Lancet*, December 1st, 1864.

From W. Vesalius Pettigrew, M.D.
I have no hesitation in stating that I never met with any medicine so efficacious as an Anti-spasmodic and Sedative. I have used it in Consumption, Asthma, Diarrhœa, and other diseases, and am perfectly satisfied with the results.

From Dr. B. J. Boulton & Co., Horncastle.
We have made pretty extensive use of Chlorodyne in our practice lately, and look upon it as an excellent Sedative and Anti-spasmodic. It seems to allay pain and irritation in whatever organ and from whatever cause. It induces a feeling of comfort and quietude not obtainable by any other remedy, and it seems to possess this great advantage over all other Sedatives, that it leaves no unpleasant after-effects.

CAUTION.— The extraordinary medical reports on the efficacy of Chlorodyne render it of vital importance that the public should obtain the genuine, which bears the words " Dr. J. Collis Browne's Chlorodyne."
Vice-Chancellor Wood stated that Dr. J. COLLIS BROWNE was undoubtedly the Inventor of CHLORODYNE ; that the whole story of the defendant Freeman was deliberately untrue.
Lord Chancellor Selborne and Lord Justice James stated that the defendant had made a deliberate misrepresentation of the decision of Vice-Chancellor Wood.
Chemists throughout the land confirm this decision that Dr. J. C. BROWNE was the Inventor of CHLORODYNE.

Sold in Bottles at 1s. 1½d., 2s. 9d., and 4s. 6d., by all Chemists.
SOLE MANUFACTURER :
J. T. DAVENPORT, 33 GREAT RUSSELL STREET, BLOOMSBURY, LONDON.

NORTH BRITISH & MERCANTILE INSURANCE COMPANY.

Established 1809.

Subscribed Capital, £2,000,000.   Paid-up Capital, £500,000.
Reserves and Balance of Undivided Profit, £1,201,243 : 5 : 11.

LIFE DEPARTMENT.

I.—Life Assurance Branch.

THE large proportion of NINE-TENTHS of the PROFITS is divided among the Policyholders on the Participating Scale every five years, and is allocated not only on the sums assured, but also on the previous additions.

The last Division of Profits was made as at 31st December 1880, when there was declared a Bonus of £1 : 7 : 6 per cent per annum.

If taken as a percentage on the original sums in the Policies, this Bonus is equivalent to an addition of from £2 : 11 : 4 per cent per annum on the oldest Policies, to £1 : 7 : 6 per cent on those now for the first time entitled to participate.

SINCE the establishment of the Company, the sum of £1,200,624 has been distributed in BONUSES.

THE ACCUMULATED FUNDS of the Life Branch, irrespective of the Paid-up Capital, amount to £3,062,174 : 6 : 1, and are specially invested to meet the obligations of that department.

THE REVENUE from Life Premiums and Interest for the year 1880 was £450,675 : 4 : 8.

II.—Annuity Branch.

ANNUITIES, Immediate, Contingent, or Deferred, are granted on favourable terms.

THE ANNUITY FUND, irrespective of the Paid-up Capital, amounts to £351,273 : 19 : 2.

FIRE DEPARTMENT.

The COMPANY INSURES against FIRE almost every description of Property, at Home or Abroad, at the lowest rates of Premium corresponding to the Risk.

THE NETT PREMIUMS for 1880 amounted to £951,173 : 10 : 5.

Every Information may be had at the Chief Offices, Branches, or Agencies.

CHIEF   { EDINBURGH   .   64 PRINCES STREET.
OFFICES { LONDON   .   61 THREADNEEDLE ST.

THE SCOTTISH
WIDOWS' FUND
Mutual Life Assurance Society

ESTABLISHED 1815.

PRESIDENT.
HIS GRACE THE DUKE OF RICHMOND AND GORDON, K.G., D.C.L. (OXON.)

VICE-PRESIDENTS.
The Right Hon. THE EARL OF HADDINGTON;
The Right Hon. THE EARL OF ROSEBERY;
The Most Hon. THE MARQUIS OF TWEEDDALE;
The Right Hon. LORD MONCREIFF, Lord Justice-Clerk.

Assurance Fund .	£7,000,000
Annual Revenue .	£900,000
Claims Paid . .	£11,000,000
Profit Divided . .	£5,500,000

Every element of Stability, Economy, and Profit is found in the Constitution and Working of the Society.

BRANCH OFFICES:

London, 28 CORNHILL. *West End Agency,* 49 PALL MALL.

Dublin, 41 WESTMORELAND STREET.	Leeds, 21 PARK ROW.
Glasgow, 114 WEST GEORGE ST.	Bristol, 40 CORN STREET.
Manchester, ALBERT SQUARE.	Belfast, 2 HIGH STREET.
Liverpool, 48 CASTLE STREET.	Newcastle, 12 GREY STREET.
Birmingham, 12 BENNETT'S HILL.	Norwich, 59 PRINCE OF WALES ROAD.

Agencies in all the important towns of the three Kingdoms.

HEAD OFFICE,
9 ST. ANDREW SQUARE, EDINBURGH,
April 1881.

SAMUEL RALEIGH, *Manager.*
A. H. TURNBULL, *Secretary.*

MUTUAL ASSURANCE with MODERATE PREMIUMS.

SCOTTISH PROVIDENT INSTITUTION
(Established 1837.)

THIS SOCIETY differs in its principles from any other Office.

INSTEAD of charging rates higher than are necessary, and afterwards returning the excess in the shape of periodical Bonuses, it gives from the first as large an Assurance as the Premiums will with safety bear—reserving the Whole Surplus for those Members who have lived long enough to secure the Common Fund from loss.

A Policy for £1200 to £1250 may thus at most ages be had for the Premium usually charged for £1000 only ; while, by reserving the surplus, large additions have been given—and may be expected in the future—on the Policies of those who live to participate.

Examples of Annual Premiums for £100 at Death (with Profits).

Age.	25	30	35	40	45	50
Payable during Life	£1 18 6	£2 1 6	£2 6 10	£2 14 9	£3 5 9	£4 1 7
Limited to 21 Payments	2 12 6	2 15 4	3 0 2	3 7 5	3 17 6	4 12 1

SUMMARY OF NEW BUSINESS IN 1880.

New Assurances—1769 for £1,054,500 were effected during the year. Premiums received, £399,538 ; Total Income, £573,609. Accumulated Funds (increased in year by £283,928), £3,918,252 : 0 : 10.

The aggregate amount of the New Assurances during the past seven years has been £7,398,025—the increase of the Realised Fund in the same period being £1,660,077.

The Result of the Investigation into the affairs of the Institution as at 31st December 1886, showed a surplus of £628,486, two-thirds of which fall to be divided among those entitled to participate ; the remaining one-third being reserved as a guarantee.

REPORTS with STATEMENT of PRINCIPLES may be had on application.

JAMES WATSON, Manager.

EDINBURGH, May 1881.

LONDON.

THE
GRAND HOTEL
TRAFALGAR SQUARE.

This Magnificent Hotel occupies the finest site in the
CENTRE OF THE METROPOLI

And combines the elegance and luxury of the most import
and attractive Hotels in Europe and America, with
repose and domestic comfort which are essentially English.

THE HOTEL stands on the site of the former Northumberland House,
commands the entire view of Trafalgar Square. It is but a short walk
distance from the Principal Public Buildings, Fine Art and other Galleri
Theatres, and Places of Amusement; and is in the midst of the means
conveyance to all parts of London and the Suburbs.

The Ground Floor is occupied by the Grand Salle à Manger, and spacio
Secondary Dining and Reception Rooms.

On the First Floor are the Ladies' Drawing Rooms, Library, and vario
Suites of Apartments, comprising all the convenience of Family Residenc
The upper Storeys contain between 200 and 300 Rooms, either *en suite* or
separate Apartments.

FOR PARTICULARS APPLY TO THE MANAGER, GRAND HOTEL,
TRAFALGAR SQUARE, LONDON.

One of the Sights and one of the Comforts of London.
THE HOLBORN RESTAURANT
218 HIGH HOLBORN.

THE FAMOUS TABLE D'HOTE DINNER, served at separate Table
accompanied with selection of high-class Music by complete Orchestra,

5.30 to 8.30 every Evening. 3s. 6d.

CPSIA information can be obtained
at www.ICGtesting.com
Printed in the USA
LVOW01s1409170816

500772LV00046B/504/P